9 - POEM. OH SMALL BEGINNINGS, YE ARE GREAT
        AND STRONG
12 - THE PEOPLE CHOSE SAUL BUT GOD CHOSE DAVID,
47 - "THE TALISMAN OF VICTORY"
63 - " THOU HAST CONQUERED, O, GALILEAN!"

David: Shepherd, Psalmist, King

67 - WE ARE ABSOLUTELY SECURE AS LONG AS WE
          ABIDE IN GOD.
   MUSIC - P. 35

99 - THE URIM AND THE THUMMIM
127 - 4 KINDS OF GREATNESS
128 - DAVID, THOUGH A PROPHET HIMSELF, SUMMONED
      OTHER PRIESTS & PROPHETS TO DETERMINE
      GOD'S WILL.
129 - ABIGAIL - A WISE & NOBLE WOMAN OF GOD
135 - NEVER ACT IN A PANIC. IF GOD'S WAY IS
      HIDDEN THEN THERE IS NO NEED FOR ACTION
154 - EQUIPOISE IN GOD
162 - THE LIVES OF GREAT MEN LIGHT UP AND INSPIRE
      OTHER LIVES
151 - THAT MOMENT DAVID KNEW THAT THE
     THUNDERCLOUD WHICH HAD BEEN SO LONG LOWERING
     OVER HIS HEAD HAD BROKEN, AND THAT THE
     EXPECTATIONS OF YEARS WERE ON THE POINT OF
     BEING REALIZED...
208 - NUMBERING THE PEOPLE

OLD TESTAMENT HEROES

DAVID: SHEPHERD, PSALMIST, KING &&

BY THE
Rev. F. B. Meyer, B.A.
Author of "The Shepherd Psalm," "Tried by Fire," "Elijah," etc., etc.

CHRISTIAN LITERATURE CRUSADE
Fort Washington, Pennsylvania 19034

CHRISTIAN LITERATURE CRUSADE
Fort Washington, Pennsylvania 19034

CANADA
Box 189, Elgin, Ontario KOG 1EO

Published in the United Kingdom by
Marshall, Morgan & Scott, Ltd.

This American edition 1977
under special arrangement with
the British publisher.

This printing 1985

ISBN 0-87508-342-0

PREFACE

THE character and life of DAVID are supremely fascinat-
ing, not only to holy souls, whose deepest thoughts
have been expressed in his unrivaled psalms, but to all men:
because of their humanness; their variety; their sharply
contrasted experiences; their exhibition of traits of generosity and courage which always elicit admiration.

While sketching every period of his life, I have concentrated myself on those passages which trace the steps by
which the shepherd became the king. It was in these that
his character was formed, his sweetest psalms composed,
and those manifold experiences encountered which enabled
him to interpret and utter the universal heart of man.

Sweet singer of the world; ancestor of Christ; founder
of a dynasty of kings; a prophet, inspired and taught, as
the Apostle Peter tells us, by the Holy Ghost; the type
and precursor of him who, though his Son, was also his
Lord; the man after God's own heart, who "did that
which was right in the eyes of the Lord, and turned not

aside from anything that he commanded him all the days of his life, save only in the matter of Uriah the Hittite." So long as time lasts DAVID must always enlist affection and command respect.

F. B. Meyer.

CONTENTS

DAVID: SHEPHERD, PSALMIST, KING

I

𝕮aken from t𝔥e 𝕾𝔥eep-𝕮otes

(I SAMUEL xvi. I.)

" We stride the river daily at its spring,
    Nor in our childish thoughtlessness foresee
What myriad vassal streams shall tribute bring,
    How like an equal it shall greet the sea.

" O small beginnings! Ye are great and strong,
    Based on a faithful heart and weariless brain;
Ye build the future fair, ye conquer wrong,
    Ye earn the crown, and wear it not in vain."
                                        J. R. LOWELL.

THE story of David opens with a dramatic contrast between the fresh hope of his young life and the rejection of the self-willed King Saul, whose course was rapidly
descending toward the fatal field of Gilboa.

Few have had a fairer chance than Saul. Choice in
gifts, goodly in appearance, favored by nature and opportunity, he might have made one of the greatest names in
history. His first exploit, the relief of Jabesh-gilead, justified the wildest anticipations of his friends. But the fair
dawn was soon overcast. The hot impatience that persisted
in offering the sacrifice before Samuel came; his needless

9

oath and ruthless proposal to take Jonathan's life; his flagrant disobedience to the distinct charge respecting Amalek—all proved that he was not fit to act as God's vicegerent, and that he must be set aside.

The final announcement of his deposition was made at Gilgal. At that spot, on entering Canaan, Israel, at Joshua's bidding, had rolled away the reproach of uncircumcision. The place suggested the only condition on which God can use human instruments; but in Saul's case there had been no humbling of pride, no submission of self-will, no putting away of the wild energy of the flesh. He was called while seeking his father's straying asses, as David was while watching his father's sheep; and there was a good deal of the wild-ass nature about Saul, as about Ishmael, which neither of them sought to subdue. Saul, it is said, rejected the word of the Lord; and the Lord rejected him from being king.

From Gilgal, Saul went up to his house at Gibeah, in the heights of Benjamin; while Samuel went to Ramah, a little to the south. There was his house; there he had judged Israel for twenty years; and there he dwelt as father and priest among the people, known far and near as the man of God (vii. 17; ix. 6, 10, 12). There, too, he mourned for Saul. No bad man drifts down the rapids unwarned, unwept; but the divine purpose cannot stay till such pitying tears are dried. Nor must we cling to the grave of the dead past, whence the Spirit of God has fled; but arise to follow as he transfers the focus of his operation from the rocky heights of Benjamin to the breezy uplands of Bethlehem, and conducts us to the house of Jesse.

In the selection of every man for high office in the service of God and man there are two sides—the divine and the human: the election of God, and its elaboration in history; the heavenly summons, and the earthly answer to its ringing notes. We must consider, therefore, I. The Root of David in God; II. The Stem of Jesse—that is, the local circumstances that might account for what the boy was; and III. The White Bud of a Noble Life.

I. The Root of David.—Once in the prophecy by Isaiah, and twice in the Book of Revelation, our Lord is called the "Root of David." "The Lion of the tribe of Judah, the Root of David, hath prevailed to open the book, and to loose the seven seals thereof." And still more emphatically, among the last words spoken by the Saviour before the curtain of the ages fell: "I Jesus am the root and the offspring of David, the bright, the morning star."

The idea suggested is of an old root, deep hidden in the earth, which sends up its green scions and sturdy stems. David's character may be considered as an emanation from the life of the Son of God before he took on himself the nature of man, and an anticipation of what he was to be and do in the fullness of time. Jesus was the Son of David, yet in another sense he was his progenitor. Thus we return to the ancient puzzle, that Jesus of Nazareth is at once David's Lord and Son (Mark xii. 35–37).

There are four great words about the choice of David, the last of which strikes deeply into the heart of that great mystery.

The Lord hath sought him a man (1 Sam. xiii. 14). No one can know the day or hour when God passes by, seeking for chosen vessels and goodly pearls. When least expecting it, we are being scrutinized, watched, tested, in daily commonplaces, to see if we shall be faithful in more momentous issues. Let us be always on the alert, our loins girt, our lamps burning, our nets mended and cleansed.

I have found David my servant (Ps. lxxxix. 20). There is ecstasy in the voice, like the thrice-repeated *found* of

Luke xv. David was found long before Samuel sent for him. Which was the moment of that blessed discovery? Was it one dawn, when in the first flicker of daylight the young shepherd led his flock from fold to pasture; or one morning, when, in an outburst of heroic faith, he rescued a trembling lamb from lion or bear; or one afternoon, when, as he sat and watched his charge, the first conception of the Shepherd Psalm stirred in his heart; or one night, when he heard the silent speech of the heavens declaring the glory of God? And was there not some secret glad response to the Master's call, like that which the disciples gave when Jesus found them at their nets and said, " Follow me " ?

He chose David to be his servant (Ps. lxxviii. 70). The people chose Saul, but God David. This made him strong. He was conscious that the purpose of God lay behind and beneath him; and when in after years Saul lay in his power, or Michal taunted him with his extravagant gestures, the thought that he was divinely commissioned was his standby (2 Sam. vii. 21). We are immovable when we touch the bed-rock of God's choice, and hear him say, " He is a chosen vessel unto me, to bear my name."

The Lord hath appointed him to be prince (1 Sam. xiii. 14). Appointments are not solely due to human patronage, nor won by human industry; they are of God. *He* bringeth low and lifteth up. Saul might chafe and fret; but from amid the ruins of his waning power the authority of David emerged as a sun from a wreck of clouds, because God willed it. Fit yourself for God's service; be faithful. He will presently appoint thee; promotion comes neither from the east nor west, but from above.

I have provided me a king (1 Sam. xvi. 1). That answers everything. The divine provision meets every need, silences every anxiety. Let us not yield to anxious forebodings for the future of the church or of our land. God has provided against all contingencies. In some unlikely quarter, in a shepherd's hut or in an artisan's cottage, God has his prepared and appointed instrument. As yet the shaft is hidden in his quiver, in the shadow of his hand; but at the precise moment at which it will tell with the greatest effect, it will be produced and launched on the air.

II. The Stem of Jesse.—We turn for a moment to consider the formative influences of David's young life. The family dwelt on the ancestral property to which Boaz, that mighty man of wealth, had brought the Rose of Moab. Perhaps it was somewhat decayed, through the exactions of the Philistine garrison, which seems to have been posted in the little town. We read of the *few* sheep in the wilderness that composed the flock; and the present sent by Jesse to his soldier sons was meager in the extreme. The conditions under which he brought up his large family of eight sons and two daughters were probably hard enough to severely tax the endurance and industry of them all.

David says nothing of his father, but twice speaks of his mother as "the handmaid of the Lord." From her he derived his poetic gift, his sensitive nature, his deeply religious character. To the father he was the lad that kept the sheep, whom it was not worth while to summon to the religious feast; to his mother he was David the beloved, and probably she first heard the psalms which have charmed and soothed the world. He honored them both with dutiful care; and when it seemed possible that they might suffer serious hurt on account of their relationship to himself, amid the pelting storm of Saul's persecution, he removed them to the safe-keeping of the king of Moab, the land of his ancestress.

The lad may have owed something to the schools of the

prophets, established by Samuel's wise prescience to maintain the knowledge of the law in Israel. They appear to have been richly endued with the gracious power of the Holy Ghost, and to have been to Israel what Iona was to the wild tribes of the North in later times. The sons of these institutions would doubtless visit Bethlehem, and find an eager response in the guileless nature of the young shepherd. From them he would learn to reduce his melodies to metrical order and accompany them with the harp; from them, too, he learned to know and prize the divine Word.

But nature was his nurse, his companion, his teacher. Bethlehem is situated six miles to the south of Jerusalem, by the main road leading to Hebron. Its site is two thousand feet above the level of the Mediterranean, on the northeast slope of a long gray ridge, with a deep valley on either side; these unite at some little distance to the east, and run down toward the Dead Sea. On the gentle slopes of the hills the fig, olive, and vine grow luxuriantly; and in the valleys are the rich corn-fields where Ruth once gleaned, and which gave the place its name, the House of Bread. The moorlands around Bethlehem, forming the greater part of the Judæan plateau, do not, however, present features of soft beauty, but are wild, gaunt, strong— character-breeding. There shepherds have always led and watched their flocks; and there David first imbibed that knowledge of natural scenery and of pastoral pursuits which colored all his after life and poetry, as the contents of the vat the dyer's hand.

Such were the schools and schoolmasters of his youth. But preëminently his spirit lay open to the Spirit of God, which brooded over his young life, teaching, quickening, and ennobling him, opening to him the books of nature and revelation, and pervading his heart with such ingenuous trust as the dumb animals of his charge reposed in him.

In the spiritual as in the physical realm he had every reason to say, long after:

> " My substance was not hid from thee
> When I was made in secret,
> And curiously wrought in the lowest parts of the earth.
> Day by day were all my members fashioned."

III. THE WHITE BUD OF A NOBLE LIFE.—He had not the splendid physique of his brother Eliab, who so impressed the aged prophet. But he was strong and athletic. His feet were nimble as a gazelle's; he could leap a wall or outstrip a troop; a bow of steel could be easily broken by his young arms; and a stone sent from his sling would hit the mark with unerring precision. Too slight to wear a man's armor, and yet able to rend a lion or bear. His face glowing with health. The blue of his eyes and beauty of his fair complexion in strong contrast to the darker visages of his companions. The sensitiveness of the poet's soul, combined with daring, resource, and power to command. His dress, a coarse and simple tunic; his accoutrements, the wallet sling, the rod and staff.

His soul is reflected in the psalms that must be attributed to this period of his life, because so free from the pressure of sorrow and anxiety, and the strife of tongues. Among them are the Eighth, Nineteenth, Twenty-third, and Twenty-ninth. So full of wonder that Jehovah should care for man, and yet so sure that he was his Shepherd; so deeply stirred by the aspect of the heavens, and yet convinced that the words of God were equally divine; so afraid of secret faults and presumptuous sins; so anxious to join in the universal chorus of praise ascending from the orchestra of nature, but yet so certain that there were yearnings and faculties within his soul in which it could not participate, and which made him its high priest and chorister. To these we will come again—they are too radiant with a light that never shone on sea or shore for us to pass them so lightly by.

Ah, guileless, blessed boy! thou little knowest that thou shalt die amid the blare of trumpets announcing the accession to the throne of thy son, the splendid Solomon; still less thou dreamest that thy unsullied nature shall one day be befouled by so sad a stain! Yet thy God loves thee, and thou shalt teach us many a lesson as we turn again the pages of thy wonderful career—poet, minstrel, soldier, exile, king—and read them in the light that streams from the face of thy greatest Son, who was born of the seed of David according to the flesh, but was declared to be the Son of God by the resurrection of the dead.

II

"From that Day Forward"

(1 Samuel xvi. 13.)

" Once for the least of children of Manasses
  God had a message and a deed to do,
  Wherefore the welcome that all speech surpasses
  Called him and hailed him greater than he knew."

F. W. H. MYERS.

FROM whatever side we view the life of David, it is remarkable. It may be that Abraham excelled him in
faith, and Moses in the power of concentrated fellowship
with God, and Elijah in the fiery force of his enthusiasm.
But none of these was so many-sided as the richly gifted
son of Jesse.

Few have had so varied a career as he: shepherd and
monarch; poet and soldier; champion of his people, and
outlaw in the caves of Judæa; beloved of Jonathan, and
persecuted by Saul; vanquishing the Philistines one day,
and accompanying them into battle on another. But in
all he seemed possessed of a special power with God and
man, which could not be accounted for by the fascination
of his manner, the beauty of his features, the rare gifts with
which his nature was dowered, or the spiritual power which
was so remarkable an attribute of his heart. We touch
these many chords, but the secret still eludes us until we
read the momentous words that sum up the result of a

17

memorable day that lay as a jewel in the obscure years of opening youth: "The Spirit of the Lord came mightily on David from that day forward."

I. It Began like Any Ordinary Day.—No angel trumpet heralded it; no faces looked out of heaven; the sun arose that morning according to his wont over the purple walls of the hills of Moab, making the cloud curtains saffron and gold. With the first glimmer of light the boy was on his way to lead his flock to pasture-lands heavy with dew. As the morning hours sped onward, many duties would engross his watchful soul—strengthening the weak, healing that which was sick, binding up that which was broken, and seeking that which was lost; or the music of his song may have thrilled the listening air. "A cunning player on the harp was he."

A breathless messenger suddenly broke upon this pastoral scene, with the tidings of Samuel's arrival at the little town, and that the prophet had refused to eat of the hastily prepared banquet until the shepherd boy had joined the bidden guests. His father had therefore sent to summon him with all speed. How the young eyes must have flashed with pleasure! Never before had he been wanted and sent for thus. Till now he had been only "the lad that kept the sheep." The family life had been complete without him. His father and brothers had followed their pursuits and pleasures in almost total disregard of the young son and brother who was destined to make their names immortal. He had borne it all in patience. His heart was not haughty, neither his eyes lofty; neither did he exercise himself in great matters or in things too high for him, but quieted himself as a child that is weaned from its mother. Still it was a genuine pleasure to feel that the family circle in great Samuel's eyes was not complete till he had come.

He therefore left his sheep with the messenger, and started at full speed for home.

Samuel, on his coming, had sanctified Jesse and his sons, passing them through a series of ceremonial ablutions to fit them for the festival in which the social and sacred elements combined. But David needed none of these. His pure and guiltless soul was right with God, and clad in the spotless robe of purity. No soil needed punctilious removal. Let us so live as to be prepared for whatever the next hour may bring forth: the spirit in fellowship with God, the robe stainlessly pure, the loins girt, the lamp trimmed. The faithful fulfilment of the commonplaces of daily life is the best preparation for any great demand that may suddenly break in upon our lives.

II. It was the Consummation of Previous Training.—We must not suppose that now for the first time the Spirit of God wrought in David's heart. To think this would indicate complete misconception of the special teaching of this incident; for Scripture always distinguishes between the regenerating and the anointing grace of the Holy Spirit. From his earliest days David had probably been the subject of his quickening and renewing work; but he had probably never experienced, before the day of which we treat, that special unction of the Holy One symbolized in the anointing oil, and indispensable for all successful spiritual work.

Our Lord was born of the Spirit; but his anointing for service did not take place till at the age of thirty, when, on the threshold of his public work, he emerged from the waters of baptism. It was to this he referred in the opening words of his earliest sermon: "The Spirit of the Lord is *upon* me, and he hath anointed me." The apostles were certainly regenerate before the day of Pentecost; but they had to wait within closed doors until they were endued with power for the conversion of men. Full often have we met with those who were unmistakably the children of God, but who had no special power in witness-bearing, nor freedom in speech, nor ability to grapple with the hearts and consciences of men. They needed what would be to them as electricity to the wire, or the spark to gunpowder. In other words, the Spirit of God has been *in*, but not *on*, them. We have seen such awake and claim the divine anointing; and suddenly they have begun to speak with new tongues, and men have not been able to resist their reasonings of sin, righteousness, and judgment to come.

This blessed anointing for service cannot be ours except there has been a previous gracious work on the heart. There must be the new life—the life of God. There must be docility, humility, fidelity to duty, cleansing from known sin, and a close walk with God. The descending flame must fall upon the whole burnt-offering of a consecrated life. And it was because all these had been wrought in David by the previous work of the Holy Spirit that he was prepared for this special unction. It may be, reader, that in the obscurity of your life, shut away from the presence of great interests, you are being prepared for a similar experience. Be careful to obey God's least prompting, whether to do or suffer, that you be prepared for the golden moment when your meek head shall be suddenly bathed in the descending chrism.

III. IT WAS MINISTERED THROUGH SAMUEL.—The old prophet had conferred many benefits on his native land, but none could compare in importance with his eager care for its youth. The creation of the schools of the prophets was due to him. Saul, in the earlier years of his manhood, felt the charm and spell of the old man's character. The stalwart sons of Jesse's house were, therefore, probably well known to him when he received the divine command to anoint one of them as Saul's successor.

Driving a heifer before him, he entered the one long street of Bethlehem and summoned the elders to a feast, so as not to arouse the suspicions of the jealous, moody king, who would not have scrupled to take his life if he had suspected the real object of his visit.

When David reached the village a strange scene met his eye. There were his father Jesse and his seven brothers, probably waiting for him in the ancestral home, preparatory to their all going together to the public banquet, to which the leading men of the village had been invited. An unusual restraint lay upon the rough tongues and harsh behavior with which Eliab and the rest were wont to treat him. At other times they would not have hesitated to express their impatience and contempt; but now the very air seemed heavy with a sacred spell that held them. No sooner had he entered, flushed with exertion, health glowing on his face, genius flashing from his eye, royalty in his mien, than the Lord said to Samuel, "Arise, anoint him: for this is he." Then Samuel took the horn of oil which he had brought with him from Nob, and poured its contents on the head of the astonished lad.

It is likely that the bystanders did not realize the significance of that act, or on the eve of the fight with Goliath Jesse would hardly have treated him so unceremoniously, and Eliab would have addressed him with more courtesy. But David probably understood. Josephus, indeed, tells us that the prophet whispered in his ear the meaning of the sacred symbol. Did the aged lips approach the young head, and, as the trembling hand pushed back the clustering locks, did they whisper in the lad's ear the thrilling words, "Thou shalt be king"? If so, in after days how they would return to him; and how vast an inspiration they would be!—a formative influence, a preparation for the great destiny that awaited him.

The descent of the oil was symbolical; in other words, it had no spiritual efficacy, but was the outward and visible sign that the Spirit of God had come mightily on the shepherd lad. For Jesus there was no oil, but instead the appearance of a dove flitting gently to its nest. For the disciples, on the day of Pentecost, there was no oil, but a flame of lambent fire alighting on each bowed head. In the process of the age these outward symbols have become mechanical and have passed from general use. We must believe that we have received when we have fulfilled the conditions of humility and the faith that claims (Gal. iii. 14).

From that memorable day David returned to his sheep; and as the months went slowly by, he must sometimes have greatly wondered when the hour of achievement would arrive. When would he have an opportunity of displaying and using his new-found force? He had to learn that we are sometimes strengthened with all might to patience and long-suffering as the prelude to heroic deeds; we have to wrestle with the lion and the bear on the hills of Bethlehem, that we may be prepared to meet Goliath in the valley of Elah.

IV. It was a Day of Rejection.—Seven of Jesse's sons were passed over. Not many wise men after the flesh, not many mighty, not many noble, were called; but God chose then, as ever, the weak, the base, the things that were despised. Seven is the perfect number; the seven sons of Jesse stand for the perfection of the flesh. This must be cut down to the ground, lest it should glory in God's presence. The lesson is hard to learn, but its acquisition is imperative. You cannot bear it? Well, be it so; then, like

Eliab, you may become one of the princes of Judah, but you shall never be God's beloved (1 Chron. xxvii. 18).

In this secret anointing of David, the first of three, we have a type of the setting apart of our Lord in the divine counsels. Rejected of men, despised of his brethren, without form or comeliness, he has been set apart as the King of the ages. As yet many a barrier lies between him and the acknowledgment which the Father has promised; but to him every knee shall bow, and every tongue shall confess that he is Lord. In the meanwhile he waits—waits till the hour of universal triumph strikes; waits till the many crowns of the destined empire meet on the head which was once encircled by the crown of thorns.

III

Summoned to the Palace

(I SAMUEL xvi. 18, 19.)

" He bowed himself
With all obedience to the king, and wrought
All kind ot service with a noble ease,
That graced the lowliest act in doing of it."
TENNYSON.

IT has been supposed that the incident we are now to consider belongs to a subsequent page in David's history,
following the narrative of the slaying of Goliath, so as to
make that the occasion of the young shepherd's first intro-
duction to Saul.   This transposition seems to be called for
by Saul's slowness to recognize his former minstrel in the
young warrior that stood before him with the head of the
Philistines' champion in his hand.

But, after all, this may be accounted for by David's
manly growth between the period of his minstrelsy and his
first great exploit in the battle-field.   How long that interval lasted we cannot tell; but during its course David had
grown from youth to manhood, his figure becoming stalwart
and robust, his face molded by the growing soul within.   If
we reject this explanation, and do not allow the incident to
remain where we find it, we have to face the further difficulty of how Saul's courtiers could dare to introduce to
their master one whose successes had already stirred his

jealousy (xviii. 9); or why it was necessary to employ so much circumlocution to describe the personality of the young singer (xvi. 18). Surely it would have been sufficient to recall what David had done in the vale of Elah to identify him at once. We hold, therefore, that this story should stand in the place it has held ever since this narrative was penned.

After his anointing David returned to his sheep. When Saul, advised by his courtiers, sent for him to charm away his melancholy, this was the specific indication he gave to Jesse, his father, "Send me David thy son, which is with the sheep." It says much for the simplicity and ingenuousness of the boy's character that he should have returned to the fold to lead and guard his helpless charge, faithfully fulfilling the routine of daily duty, and waiting for God to do what Samuel had spoken to him of. So Jesus left the temple, where to his boyish eyes a radiant glimpse had been afforded of doing his Father's business, to be subject to his parents and engage in the humble toils of the carpenter's shop.

A contemporary hand has given a brief portraiture of his character as it presented itself at this period to casual observers. One of Saul's young men said, "Behold, I have seen a son of Jesse the Bethlehemite, that is cunning in playing, and a mighty man of valor, and a man of war, and prudent in speech, and a comely person, and the Lord is with him." These five characteristics enable us to form a graphic conception of the young hero who was making the country-side ring with his renown.

I. The Minstrel.—He had the poetic temperament, sensitive to nature, open to every impression from mountain and vale, from dawn and eve; and he had besides the power of translating his impressions into speech and song.

His psalms commemorate to the present day, and will as
long as man shall live, the story of the green strips of
meadow-land where his flocks grazed at noon; the little
stream somewhere near Bethlehem of whose. limpid waters
they drank; the smooth paths which he selected for their
feet; the rocky defiles where they were in danger of lion
and bear.

A great modern poet imagines him reciting, as he sang to
his harp, his call to his sheep, the song of the autumn vin-
tage, the joyous marriage lay, the solemn funeral dirge, the
chant of the Levites as they performed their sacred duties,
the marching music of the men of Bethlehem when they
repelled some border foray.   And we might add to these
his marvelous power in depicting the sacred hush of dawn,
where there is neither speech nor language, just before the
sun leaps up as a bridegroom to run his race; and the solemn pomp of night, where worlds beyond worlds open to
the wondering gaze.   And to these we might add the marvelous description of the thunder-storms that broke over
Palestine, rolling peal after peal, from the great waters of
the Mediterranean, over the cedars of Lebanon, to the far-
distant wilderness of Kadesh, until the sevenfold thunders
are followed by torrents of rain, and these by the clear
shining in which Jehovah blesses his people with peace
(Ps. xxiii., xix., viii., xxix.).

The psalm began with David.   Its lyric beauty and tender grace; its rhythmic measure; its exuberant halleluiahs
and plaintive lamentations; its inimitable expression of the
changeful play of light and shade over the soul; its blending of nature and godliness; its references to the life of men
and the world, as regarded from the standpoint of God—
these elements in the Psalter, which have endeared it to holy
souls in every age, owe their origin to the poetic, heaven-
touched soul of the sweet singer of Israel.   What wonder

that Saul's young man said that he was cunning in playing!
The psalms which he composed in those early days—and
which are so delightfully free from the darker elements
which persecution and unkindness and consciousness of
sin introduced into the later creation of his genius—were
destined to go singing through the world, working on men
effects like those wrought on the king, of whom it is said
that when David took the harp and played with his hand,
Saul was refreshed.

II. THE YOUNG WARRIOR.—There was abundant opportunity for the education of his prowess. The Philistines'
frontier was not far away from his native town; and probably there were many repetitions of the incident of after
years, when the sons of the alien held it, and placed a guard
demanding toll of the water of the well of Bethlehem that
was by the gate. Many a skirmish had the men of Bethlehem with the border warriors, who would sweep down
upon the produce of their vineyards and corn-fields when
the harvest was ripe. In these David acquired the character of being a man of valor and a mighty man of war. It
may be that sometimes he had to stand alone against a
handful of sheep-stealers intent on plundering the fold.

He tells us how he needed to be on the alert against the
wild beasts that prowled among the hills of Judah—the lion
with his hungry teeth, the bear with his deadly hug. For
these he had no fear. He smote them, and delivered the
trembling lambs from their mouth. He caught them by
their beard and slew them. He could break a bow of steel
with those strong young arms, and wield Goliath's sword
with ease; or club a wild beast with his staff, and hurl a
stone with unerring aim. A proud young Samson, laugh-
ing in the fullness of his manly strength.

But he would have been the last to attribute his exploits

to his sinewy strength.   By faith he had learned to avail himself of the might of God.   Was he not his servant, designated for a great mission, summoned to wage uncompromising war with the uncircumcised?   He might be a babe; yet out of his mouth God had established strength, in order to still the enemy and the avenger!   He might be a suckling; yet he was made to have dominion over the works of God's hands!   Listen to his buoyant challenge:

> " For by thee have I run through a troop;
> And by my God have I leaped over a wall. . . .
> It is God that girdeth me with strength. . . .
> He maketh my feet like hinds' feet. . . .
> He teacheth my hands to war. . . .
> Thou hast subdued under me those that rose up against me."

Through faith he subdued kingdoms, stopped the mouths of lions, escaped the edge of the sword, waxed mighty in war, turned to flight armies of aliens.

III. PRUDENT IN SPEECH.—The sagacity of David will appear as our story proceeds. He was as prudent to advise and scheme as he was swift to execute. He had understanding of the times, of human hearts, of wise policy; and he knew just how and when to act. Frank to his friends, generous to his foes, constant in his attachments, calm in danger, patient in trouble, chivalrous and knightly, he had every element of a born leader of men, and was equally at home in the counsels of the state and the decisions of the battle-field. Whatever emergency threatened, he seemed to know just how to meet it. And this was no doubt due to the repose of his spirit in God. The sad mistakes he made may be traced to his yielding to the sway of impulse and passion, to his forgetfulness of his habit of drawing near unto God, and inquiring of him before taking any important step. The attitude of his soul is sweetly mirrored in one of his earliest psalms:

> " O my Strength, I will wait upon thee. . . .
> Unto thee, O my Strength, will I sing praises."

When men live like that, they cannot fail to be prudent in speech, sagacious in counsel.

IV. THE CHARM OF HIS PRESENCE.—He was David the beloved. Wherever he moved he cast the spell of his personal magnetism. Saul yielded to it, and thawed; the servants of the royal household loved him; Michal, Saul's daughter, loved him; the soul of Jonathan was knit with his soul; the women of Israel forgot their loyalty to Saul as they sounded the praises of the young hero who was so goodly to look upon; the wild, rough soldiers were willing to risk their lives in order to gratify his wish for a draft from Bethlehem's well. So he passed through life, swaying the scepter of irresistible potency over men and women. The beautiful Abigail is glad to wash the feet of his servants; Achish says that he is an angel of the Lord; Ittai the Gittite clings to him in his exile; the people slink into the city because he is weeping over Absalom; when he speaks, the hearts of the men of Judah, conscious of treachery, and backward to welcome him, are moved even as the heart of one man. Beloved of God and man, with a heart tremulous to the touch of love, the soil of his soul was capable of bearing crops to enrich the world; but it was also capable of the keenest suffering possible to man.

V. GOD WAS WITH HIM.—He had no hesitation in describing himself as " thy servant," liable to hidden and presumptuous faults, from which he desired above all things to be delivered. He thought of God as his Rock, Redeemer,

Shepherd, and Host in the house of life, his Comforter in every darksome glen. In weariness he found green pastures; in thirst, still waters; in perplexity, righteous guidance; in danger, sure defense—in what the Lord was to his soul. God's Word, though he knew but a part of it, was perfect, right, pure; and as he recited it to himself, under great nature's tent, it restored his soul, rejoiced his heart, enlightened his eyes, and seemed better than the honey that dripped from the rock. He set the Lord always before him; because he was at his right hand, he could not be moved; and therefore his heart was glad.

IV

𝔄 𝔇𝔞𝔯𝔨 𝔅𝔞𝔠𝔨𝔤𝔯𝔬𝔲𝔫𝔡

(1 SAMUEL xvii. 11.)

> " I flung away
> Those keys that might have open set
> The golden sluices of the day;
> But clutch the keys of darkness yet.
> I hear the reapers singing go
> Into God's harvest; I that might
> With them have chosen, here below
> Grope shuddering at the gates of night."
>
> J. R. LOWELL.

A GREAT contrast, as we have said, is evidently intended by the historian between Saul and David. The portrait of Saul is drawn in Rembrandt colors, to set forth the excelling beauty of God's designated king.

The king of Israel took his first step away from God when he permitted himself to be betrayed into undue haste and precipitation, and offered the burnt-offering at Michmash before Samuel came. He took further steps in the same direction in the outburst of indignation against Jonathan for violating his regulation about abstinence from food. But the final break took place when he disobeyed the distinct command of Jehovah through his prophet, and spared Agag and the choice of the spoil. Then he rejected the word of the Lord, and God gave him up to his own evil heart. From that moment his course was always downward

toward the gathering gloom of Gilboa.   From the disobedi-
ent heart God withdraws his keeping power; and as it is no
longer tenanted by the Spirit of the Most High, it becomes
at once the prey and habitation of unclean spirits, remind-
ing us of the awful words with which Isaiah describes the
desolation of Edom (Isa. xxxiv. 14, 15, R.V.).

Such was the state of Saul's heart. Since he was not willing to retain God in his knowledge, God gave him up to a
reprobate mind, to do those things which are not fitting.

We will notice some points in Saul's dark eclipse which
will serve to illustrate salient features in the young shepherd's character.

I. FORSAKEN BY THE SPIRIT OF GOD.—Browning con-
ceives of him amid the black mid-tent's silence, from which
for days together not a sound came to the anxious watch-
ers; the blackness of darkness reigning; within, the figure
of Saul resting against the tent-prop, without movement,
speech, or appetite for food; shuddering for a moment
under the first spell of music, and then resuming his insen-
sibility to all.

The departure of the Spirit of the Lord probably refers to
that special equipment for the regal office which had once
come mightily upon him.   In his case it had rather to do
with office than with any change of disposition and heart
(1 Sam. x. 10; xi. 6).   By his wilfulness and disobedience
Saul forfeited this royal prerogative. The light faded off
his soul, and he became as other men.

Nothing in this world or the next can be compared for
horror to the withdrawal of God from us. It involves the
perdition of body and soul, because it is the one force by
which evil is restrained and good fostered.   Take the sun
from the center of the solar system, and each planet, breaking from its leash, would pursue a headlong course, collid-

ing with the rest, and dashing into the abyss. So when God's presence is lost, every power in the soul rises in revolt. Ah! bitter wail, when a man realizes the true measure of the calamity which has befallen him, and cries with Saul, " I am sore distressed; for God is departed from me, and answereth me no more."

It is a very serious thing to ask if we are not tampering with the Spirit of the Lord. To do so will turn the most radiant dawn into the chill twilight of a wintry day when the blizzard fills the air with snow and ice. Beware lest you fret against the divine delays, or disobey the divine command. Know in this thy day the things that belong to thy peace, lest they be forever hid from thy view; and, as the sun's last rim sinks beneath the waves, the storm-clouds of jealousy, superstition, frenzy, bear down in thick battalions.

How different with David! The Lord was with him. To the clear, bright eye of his faith the living God was more real than the giant that stalked each morning before the hosts of Israel. Had he not delivered him from the paw of the lion and from the paw of the bear? And was he not as real amid the dignity of the court or the clash of the battle-field? The dew of the divine blessing rested upon that fair young head, and the light of the Shechinah shone from the inner shrine through those clear blue eyes. With him the Spirit of God was not simply an equipment of gift for service, but the resident presence of the divine in soul and heart.

II. TROUBLED BY AN EVIL SPIRIT FROM THE LORD.—Evidently the conception is of Jehovah surrounded by spirits, some good and some evil. He has only to speak, and one powerful to exercise a malign and deadly influence hastens to do his bidding. Micaiah spoke after the same manner in the dark hour of Ahab's infatuation (1 Kings

xxii. 19–23). This method of speech is unfamiliar. We prefer to say that God permits evil spirits to fasten on souls which have refused him, as vultures on the carcass from which life has fled. We go further, and say that God always means to do the best by every creature that he has made; but that we have the power of extracting evil from his good; of transforming his sunshine and rain into hemlock and deadly nightshade and rank poison; of transmuting the roses which fall from his hand into the red-hot cinders that scorch and burn into the flesh.

Never doubt that God is good; that he sends good and gentle spirits to stay man from his purpose and conduct him into the light of life; but when we turn against God it seems as though he has commenced to be our enemy, and to fight against us; the reality being that whereas we once went with the stream of the divine blessing, we are now wading against it with difficulty and peril. With the froward God shows himself froward; and with the perverse, his angels, conscience, gratitude, the memory of the past, convictions of duty, intended to elevate and save, oppose their progress as mortal foes. They wrestle with us—or, rather, we wrestle with them—in the dark night, in which we cannot distinguish friend from foe. So when Judas had finally chosen to betray our Lord, the very pleadings of Jesus hardened his heart and sealed his doom.

With David, on the other hand, the Spirit of God was constantly coöperating. He lived and walked in fellowship with the unseen. All the genial influences of heaven, as they fell upon his young spirit, elicited responses of love and faith, like the strains of music which each passing breeze summons from the Æolian lyre.

III. SAUL'S DISCORD.—The fact that music was the corrective of the king's malady seems to indicate that, being wrong with God, he was out of harmony with the universe, which is the circumference of which God is center. It is impossible to define music. In its grander and more lovely strains it has escaped the defiling touch of sin, and is, so to speak, the echo of eternity; spray from the waves of light and glory that break upon our shores; the expression of the infinite order and rhythm of the spheres. Music, there-fore, is the natural expression of the perfect life and peace of heaven. There the harpers harp upon their harps; there redeemed and glorified spirits raise new songs; there holy beings express their perfect accord with the nature of God and the order of the universe in outbursts of harmonious sound. Perfected sense, which can only be had on the con-dition of unbroken union with God's will, purpose, and life, would detect all things uttering " Halleluiah!" and be com-pelled by the contagiousness of a holy sympathy to swell the anthem.

To all this Saul was a stranger. He was out with God, and there was consequently discord in his heart and life. Music falling on his ear recalled memories of his former bet-ter self, and laid a brief spell upon the discordant elements of his soul, reducing them to a momentary order, destined, however, to be marred and spoiled so soon as the sweet sounds were withdrawn. Yes, it is ever thus. If you have not received the at-one-ment, if you are not at peace with God through Jesus Christ, you are at enmity, by wicked works and inward temper; and there can be, therefore, no sympathy between you and the universe around. Art, music, the engagements of daily business, the whirl of society, the exercises of religion, may do what David's harp did for Saul, in producing a momentary stillness and sense of harmony with your environment. But it is only for a moment; when the spell is withdrawn, the olden spirit of disorder asserts itself.

With David, on the other hand, the harp was the symbol of a soul at rest in God. All things were, therefore, his; all spoke to his soul of the harmonies subsisting in the unseen and eternal world. And it was because his own spirit was so perfectly harmonious with the nature of God and with the universe that he could cast the spell of calming and quieting influence over another. This may explain the influence of music in all ages of the world over the maladies of the soul. Elisha called for a minstrel to calm his disquieted spirit. Pythagoras, as Seneca tells us, was in the habit of quieting the troubles of his mind with a harp. Philip V. of Spain was recalled from the profoundest melancholy by the famous singer Farinelli. The servants of Saul were therefore justified in urging him, in one of his lucid moments, to permit them to seek out a man who was a cunning player on the harp. And the power that David exercised over him is an illustration of a similar charm which we may individually exert upon the restless, storm-tossed spirits around us. Let us accept God's basis of the reconciliation. Let us stand beneath the cross, which is the center of reconciliation from the discords of sin, till we are in perfect accord with it; and let us go forth to induce men to come to that center also, to be reconciled to God, and to learn the mystery of that peace of which Jesus spoke on the eve of his death and the day of his resurrection.

IV. SAUL'S UNBELIEF.—If a man is wrong with God, faith is impossible; for it is the health-bloom of the soul. When, therefore, Goliath stalked through the valley of Elah and defied the armies of Israel, Saul was greatly afraid. Where was now the prowess that engaged the early love and admiration of the people, that delivered Jabesh-gilead, and that vexed the foes of Israel whithersoever he turned himself? It had vanished, as the beauty passes from the surface of the fruit which is rotten at the core, and as the forms of the hills disappear from ruffled water. Under happier conditions he would have become the champion of his people; now he cowered in his tent.

To David, on the other hand, there was no such fear. His soul was full of God. He was his light and salvation; whom should he fear? the strength of his life; of whom should he be afraid? He was hidden in the secret of God's pavilion, and abode under the shadow of the Almighty. There was no unsteadiness in the hand that slung the stone, no tremor in the heart. He was strong in faith, because his young heart was pure and good and right, and in living fellowship with Jehovah.

V

𝔗𝔥𝔢 𝔉𝔞𝔦𝔱𝔥 𝔬𝔣 𝔊𝔬𝔡'𝔰 𝔈𝔩𝔢𝔠𝔱

(1 SAMUEL xvii.)

"Who the line
Shall draw, the limits of the power define
That even imperfect faith to man affords?"
WORDSWORTH.

IN the valley of Elah to-day the traveler finds the remains of an immense terebinth. Perhaps this gave it
its name, "the valley of the terebinth."   Starting from the
neighborhood of the ancient city of Hebron, the valley runs
in a northwesterly direction toward the sea; it is about a
mile across, and in the middle there is a deep ravine, some
twenty feet across, with a depth of ten or twelve feet.
Winter torrents have made this their track.

Having recovered from the chastisement inflicted on
them by Saul and Jonathan at Michmash, the Philistines
had marched up the valley of Elah, encamping on its western slope between Shochoh and Ephes-dammim; a name
with an ominous meaning—"the boundary of blood"—
probably because on more than one occasion it had been
the scene of border forays.   Saul pitched his camp on the
other side of the valley; behind them the Judæan hills, ridge
on ridge, to the blue distance where Jerusalem lay, as yet
in the hands of the Jebusite.   That valley was to witness
an encounter which brought into fullest contrast the princi-

ples on which God's warriors are to contend—not only with
flesh and blood, but against the principalities and powers of
darkness. Three figures stand out sharply defined on that
memorable day.

First, *the Philistine champion.* He was tall—nine feet
six inches in height; he was heavily armed, for his armor
fell a spoil to Israel, was eagerly examined and minutely
described; they even weighed it, and found it five thousand
shekels of brass, equivalent to two hundredweight; he was
protected by an immense shield, borne by another in front
of him, so as to leave his arms and hands free; he wielded
a ponderous spear, while sword and javelin were girt to his
side; he was apt at braggadocio, talked of the banquet he
proposed to give to the fowls and beasts, and defied the
armies of the living God.

Second, *Saul*—a choice young man and a goodly. There
was not among the children of Israel a goodlier person than
he; from his shoulders and upward he was higher than any
of the people. He had also a good suit of armor, a helmet
of brass, and a coat of mail. In earlier days, when he had
blown the trumpet, its notes had rung throughout the land,
stirring all hearts with anticipations of certain victory.
Even now the formula of his former faith and fervor came
easily to his lips, as he assured the young shepherd that the
Lord would certainly be with him; but he dared not ad-
venture himself in conflict with what he reckoned were
utterly overwhelming odds. He was near daunting David
with his materialism and unbelief: "Thou art not able to
go against this Philistine to fight with him: for thou art but
a youth, and he a man of war from his youth."

Third, *David.* He was but a youth, and ruddy, and
withal of a fair countenance. No sword was in his hand;
he carried a staff—probably his shepherd's crook; no
armor had he on, save the breastplate of righteousness and

the helmet of salvation; no weapon but a sling in his hand, and five smooth stones, which he had chosen out of the torrent bed, and put in the shepherd's bag which he had, even in his scrip. But he was in possession of a mystic spiritual power, which the mere spectator might have guessed, but which he might have found it difficult to define. The living God was a reality to him. His countrymen were not simply, as Goliath insinuated, servants to Saul; they were the army of the living God. When he spake of armies, using the plural as of more than one, he may have been thinking of Jacob's vision of the host of angels at Mahanaim; or of Joshua's, when the Angel of the Covenant revealed himself as Captain of the Lord's host that waited unseen under arms, prepared to coöperate with that which Israel's chieftain was about to lead across the Jordan. As likely as not, to the lad's imagination the air was full of horses and chariots of fire; of those angel hosts which in after days he addressed as strong in might, harkening unto the voice of God, and hastening to do his pleasure in all places of his dominion. At least he had no doubt that the Lord would vindicate his glorious name, and deliver into his hands this uncircumcised Philistine.

Let us study the origin and temper of this heroic faith.

I. It had been Born in Secret and Nursed in Solitude.—As day after day he considered the heavens and earth, they appeared as one vast tent, in which God dwelt. Nature was the material dwelling-place of the eternal Spirit, who was as real to his young heart as the works of his hands to his poet's eyes. God was as real to him as Jesse or his brothers or Saul or Goliath. His soul had so rooted itself in this conception of God's presence that he bore it with him, undisturbed by the shout of the soldiers as they went forth to the battle, and the searching questions addressed to him by Saul.

This is the unfailing secret. There is no short cut to the life of faith, which is the all-vital condition of a holy and victorious life. We must have periods of lonely meditation and fellowship with God. That our souls should have their mountains of fellowship, their valleys of quiet rest beneath the shadow of a great rock, their nights beneath the stars, when darkness has veiled the material and silenced the stir of human life, and has opened the view of the infinite and eternal, is as indispensable as that our bodies should have food. Thus alone can the sense of God's presence become the fixed possession of the soul, enabling it to say repeatedly, with the psalmist, " Thou art near, O God."

II. IT HAD BEEN EXERCISED IN LONELY CONFLICT.—
With a beautiful modesty David would probably have kept to himself the story of the lion and the bear, unless it had been extracted from him by a desire to magnify Jehovah. Possibly there had been many conflicts of a similar kind; so that his faith had become strengthened by use, as the sinews of his wiry young body by exertion. In these ways he was being prepared for this supreme conflict.

What we are in solitude we shall be in public. Do not for a moment suppose, O self-indulgent disciple, that the stimulus of a great occasion will dower thee with a heroism of which thou betrayest no trace in secret hours. The crisis will only reveal the true quality and temper of the soul. The flight at the Master's arrest will make it almost needless for the historian to explain that the hour which should have been spent in watching was squandered in sleep. It is the universal testimony of holy men that lonely hours are fullest of temptation. It is in these we must conquer if we would be victorious when the eyes of some great assembly are fastened upon us.

III. It Stood the Test of Daily Life.—There are some who appear to think that the loftiest attainments of the spiritual life are incompatible with the grind of daily toil and the friction of the home. " Emancipate us from these," they cry; " give us nothing to do except to nurse our souls to noble deeds; deliver us from the obligations of family ties, and we will fight for those poor souls who are engrossed with the cares and ties of the ordinary and commonplace."

It was not thus with David. When Jesse, eager to know how it fared with his three elder sons, who had followed Saul to the battle, bade David take them rations, and a present to the captain of their division, there was an immediate and ready acquiescence in his father's proposal: " He rose up early in the morning, and took, and went, as Jesse had commanded him." And before he left his flock he was careful to intrust it with a keeper. We must always watch not to neglect one duty for another; if we are summoned to the camp, we must first see to the tendance of the flock. He that is faithful in the greater must first have been faithful in the least. It is in the home, at the desk, and in the Sunday-school that we are being trained for service at home and abroad. We must not forsake the training-ground till we have learned all the lessons God has designed it to teach, and have heard his summons.

IV. It Bore Meekly Misconstruction and Rebuke. —Reaching the camp, he found the troops forming in battle array, and ran to the front. He had already discovered his brothers, and saluted them, when he was arrested by the braggart voice of Goliath from across the valley, and saw, to his chagrin, the men of Israel turn to flee, stricken with

sore affright. When he expressed surprise, he learned from
bystanders that even Saul shared the general panic, and
had issued rewards for a champion. So he passed from
one group to another of the soldiery, questioning, gathering
further confirmation of his first impressions, and evincing
everywhere the open-eyed wonder of his soul that " any
man's heart should fail because of him."

Eliab had no patience with the words and bearing of his
young brother. How dare he suggest that the behavior of
the men of Israel was unworthy of themselves and their religion! What did he mean by inquiring so minutely after
the particulars of the royal reward ? Was he thinking of
winning it? It was absurd to talk like that! Of course it
could only be talk; but it was amazing to hear it suggested
that he too was a soldier and qualified to fight. Evidently
something should be said to thrust him back into his right
place, and minimize the effect of his words, and let the bystanders know who and what he was. " Why art thou come
down? With whom," he said with a sneer, " hast thou left
those few sheep in the wilderness? " Ah, what venom, as
of an asp, lay in those few words! David, however, ruled
his spirit, and answered softly. " Surely," said he, " my
father's wish to learn of your welfare was cause enough to
bring me here." It was there that the victory over Goliath
was really won. To have lost his temper in this unpro-
voked assault would have broken the alliance of his soul
with God, and drawn a veil over his sense of his presence.
But to meet evil with good, and maintain an unbroken
composure, not only showed the burnished beauty of his
spirit's armor, but cemented his alliance with the Lamb of
God.

To bear with unfailing meekness the spiteful attacks of
malice and envy; not to be overcome by evil, but to overcome evil with good; to suffer wrong; to possess one's soul

in patience; to keep the mouth with a bridle when the wicked is before us; to pass unruffled and composed through a very cyclone of unkindliness and misrepresentation—this is only possible to those in whose breasts the dove-like Spirit has found an abiding-place, and whose hearts are sentineled by the peace of God; and these are they who bear themselves as heroes in the fight. A marvelous exhibition was given that day in the valley of Elah that those who are gentlest under provocation are strongest in the fight, and that meekness is really an attribute of might.

V. It Withstood the Reasonings of the Flesh.— Saul was very eager for David to adopt his armor, though he dared not don it himself. He was taken with the boy's ingenuous earnestness, but advised him to adopt the means. "Don't be rash; don't expect a miracle to be wrought. By all means trust God, and go; but be wise. We ought to adopt ordinary precautions."

It was a critical hour. Had David turned aside to act on these suggestions he would certainly have forfeited the divine alliance, which was conditioned by his guileless faith. There is no sin in using means; but they must come second, not first; they must be such as God suggests. It is a sore temptation to adopt them as indicated by the flesh, and hope that God will bless them, instead of waiting before him to know what he would have done, and how. Many a time has the advice of worldly prudence damped the eager aspiration of the spirit, and hindered the doing of a great deed.

But an unseen hand withdrew David from the meshes of temptation. He had already yielded so far to Saul's advice as to have donned his armor and girded on the sword. Then he turned to Saul and said, "I cannot go with these;" and he put them off him. It was not now Saul's armor *and* the Lord, but the Lord alone; and he was able, without hesitation, to accost the giant with the words, "The Lord saveth not with sword and spear."

His faith had been put to the severest tests and was approved. Being more precious than silver or gold, it had been exposed to the most searching ordeal; but the furnace of trial had shown it to be of heavenly temper. Now let Goliath do his worst; he shall know that there is a God in Israel.

VI

"In the Name of the Lord of Hosts"

(I SAMUEL xvii. 45.)

> " Oh, I have seen the day
> When, with a single word,
> God helping me to say,
> ' My trust is in the Lord,'
> My soul hath quenched a thousand foes,
> Fearless of all that could oppose."
>
> COWPER.

WHILE the two armies, on either side of the ravine, waited expectant, every eye was suddenly attracted by the slight young figure which, staff in hand, emerged from the ranks of Israel and descended the slope. For a little while David was hid from view, as he bent intent on the pebbles that lined the bottom, of which five smooth stones were presently selected and placed in his shepherd's bag. Then, to the amazement of the Philistines, and especially of their huge champion, he sprang up on the further bank and rapidly moved toward him.

Goliath had apparently been sitting; and when he realized that the youth was daring to accept his challenge he arose, and came, and drew near to meet David, cursing him as he did so, and threatening him that his blood should encrimson the mountain sward, while his unburied body feasted the wild things of earth and air. "Then said David to the Philistine, Thou comest to me with a sword,

and with a spear, and with a javelin: but I come to thee
in the name of the Lord of hosts, the God of the armies of
Israel, whom thou hast defied."

I. The Talisman of Victory.—"The name of the
Lord of hosts." Throughout the Scriptures a name is not
simply, as with us, a label; it is a revelation of character.
It catches up and enshrines some moral or physical pecu-
liarity in which its owner differs from other men, or which
constitutes his special gift and force. The names which
Adam gave the animals that were brought to him were
founded on characteristics which struck his notice. And
the names which the second Adam gave to the apostles
either expressed qualities which lay deep within them, and
which he intended to evolve, or unfolded some great purpose for which they were being fitted.

Thus the name of God, as used so frequently by the
heroes and saints of sacred history, stands for those divine
attributes and qualities which combine to make him what
he is. In the history of the early church *the Name* was a
kind of summary of all that Jesus had revealed of the nature
and the heart of God. "For the sake of the Name they
went forth, taking nothing of the Gentiles." There was no
need to specify whose name it was—there was none other
name by which men could be saved, none other name that
could be compared with that, or mentioned on the same
page. Stars die out and become invisible when the sun
appears. That name is above every name, and in it every
knee shall bow, and every tongue confess; because it em-
bodies under one all-sufficient designation everything that
any single soul, or the whole race, can require or imagine
or attain in the conceiving of God.

The special quality that David extracted from the bundle
of qualities represented by the divine name of God is indi-

cated in the words, *the Lord of hosts*. That does not mean
only that God was Captain of the embattled hosts of Israel;
that idea was expressed in the words that followed: "The
God of the armies of Israel." But there was probably something of this sort in David's thought: he conceived of angels
and worlds, of the armies of heaven and the elements of matter, of winds and waves, of life and death, as a vast ordered
army, obedient to the commands of their Captain, Jehovah
of hosts. In fact, his idea was identical with that of the
heathen centurion of the Gospels, who said he was a man
under authority, having servants to whom he said, "Come,"
or "Go," or "Do this or that."

To come in the name of the Lord of hosts did not simply mean that David understood Jehovah to be all this,
but implied his own identification by faith with all that was
comprehended in this sacred name. An Englishman in a
foreign land occupies a very different position, and speaks
in a very different tone, according to whether he assumes a
private capacity as an ordinary traveler, or acts as representative and ambassador of his country. In the former
case he speaks in his own name, and receives what respect
and obedience it can obtain; in the latter he is conscious
of being identified with all that is associated with the term
"Great Britain." For a man to speak in the name of England means that England speaks through his lips; that the
might of England is ready to enforce his demands; and
that every sort of power which England wields is pledged to
avenge any affront or indignity to which he may be exposed.

Thus, when Jesus bids us ask what we will in his name,
he means, not that we should simply use that name as an
incantation or formula, but that we should be so one with
him in his interests, purposes, and aims that it should be as
though he were himself approaching the Father with the
petitions we bear.

There is much for us to learn concerning this close identification with God before we shall be able to say, with David, " I come to thee in the name of the Lord of hosts." It is only possible to those who carefully fulfil certain conditions which were familiar enough to this God-taught youth. But it were well worth our while to withdraw ourselves from the activities of our life, to lay aside everything that might hinder the closeness of our union with the divine nature and interests, and to become so absolutely identified with God that his name might be our strong tower, our refuge, our battle-cry, our secret of victory.   Oh, to be able to approach each high-handed wrong-doer, each confederacy of evil, each assault of the powers of darkness, each tribe of savages, each drink-sodden district, each congregation of the unsaved and impenitent, with the words, " I come in the name of the Lord of hosts " !

II. THE CONDITIONS ON WHICH WE ARE WARRANTED IN USING THE NAME.— 1. *When we are pure in our motives.* There was no doubt as to the motive which prompted David to this conflict.   It is true that he had spoken to the men of Israel, saying, " What shall be done to the man that killeth this Philistine?" but no one supposed that he acted as he did because of the royal reward.   His one ambition was to take away the reproach from Israel, and to let all the earth know that there was a God in Israel.

We must be wary here.   It is so easy to confuse issues which are wide asunder as the poles, and to suppose that we are contending for the glory of God when we are really combating for our church, our cause, our prejudices or opinions.   It has always been a temptation to earnest men to veil from their own eyes the selfishness of their motives and aims by insisting, with vehement asseveration, that they are actuated by pure zeal for the cause of God.

To fall into this sin, though unconsciously, is to forfeit the right to use his sacred name. We may still conjure with it and invoke it, but in vain. The very demons we seek to bind as with a spell will deride us, and leap out on us, and chase us before them. How constantly we need to expose our hearts to the inspiration of the Holy Spirit, that he may wholly cleanse them, and fill them with an all-consuming devotion to the glory of God; so that the words may be true of us, as of our Lord, "The zeal of thy house hath eaten me up"!

2. *When we are willing to allow God to occupy his right place.* David said repeatedly that the whole matter was God's. He might gather up the spoils of the battle, but the overthrow of Goliath and the Philistine host was not in his province at all. "The battle is the Lord's. . . . This day will the Lord deliver thee into mine hand. . . . The Lord saveth, and he will give you into our hands."

And David's attitude has been that of every man who has wrought great exploits in the behalf of righteousness. Moses said, "The Lord hath appeared unto me, and he will bring you up out of the affliction of Egypt." Samuel said, "Prepare your hearts unto the Lord, and he will deliver you out of the hand of the Philistines." Paul said, " I will not dare to speak of any things save those which Christ wrought through me." We must recognize Jesus Christ as the essential warrior, worker, organizer, and administrator of his church, through the Holy Spirit. Whatever is rightly done, he must do. We are not called to work for him, but to let him work through us. Of him and through him and to him are all things. The battle is not ours, but his. His skill must direct us; his might empower us; his uplifted hands bring us victory.

3. *When we take no counsel with the flesh.* It must have **been** a hard thing for a youth to oppose his opinion to

Saul's, especially when the king was so solicitous for his welfare. "Spare thyself, my son," he seemed to say; "be wise; take ordinary precautions; do not throw thy young life away." It was a dangerous moment. To meet scorn, hatred, wrong-doing with uncompromising defiance and resistance is so much easier than to refuse assistance or advice which is kindly meant. It was well for him, indeed, that David withstood the siren song and remained unaffected by the blandishments of royal favor. He could not have served two masters so utterly antagonistic. To have yielded to Saul would have put him beyond the fire-ring of the divine environment.

How perpetually does Satan breathe into our ears the soft words that Peter whispered to his Master when he began to speak about the cross: "Spare thyself: that shall not come unto thee"! There is so much talk about the legitimacy of means that no room is left on which the Almighty can act. Means are right enough in their right place; but that place is far from first. Both their nature and time have to be fixed by Him who refuses helmets of brass and coats of mail, that no flesh should glory in his presence, but who uses the rustic sling, the smooth stone from the brook, and the sword of Goliath.

III. The Bearing of Those who Use the Name.—
1. *They are willing to stand alone.* The lad asked no comradeship in the fight. There was no running to and fro to secure a second. He was perfectly prepared to bear the whole brunt of the fray without sympathy or succor, so sure was he that the Lord of hosts was with him, and that the God of Jacob was his refuge.

2. *They are deliberate.* He was free from the nervous trepidation which so often unfits us to play our part in some great scene. Our heart will throb so quickly, our

movements become so fitful and unsteady. Calmly and quietly he went down the slope and selected the pebbles which best suited his purpose. In this quietness and confidence he found his strength. His mind was kept in perfect peace, because it was stayed on God. He did not go by haste or flight, because the Lord went before him, and the Holy One of Israel was his rearward.

3. *They are fearless.* When the moment came for the conflict, David did not hesitate, but ran toward the Philistine army to meet their champion. There was no fear of the result in that young heart; no tremor in the voice that answered the rough taunt; no falter in the arm that wielded the sling; no lack of precision in the aim that drove the stone to the one part of the Philistine's body that was unprotected and vulnerable.

4. *They are more than conquerors.* The stone sank into the giant's forehead; in another moment he fell stunned to the earth. There was no time to lose before he could recover himself, or his friends so far overcome by their stupefied amazement; his head had been hewn from his body by one blow of his own sword. And when the Philistines saw that their champion was dead, they fled. The spoils of victory lay with the victor. David took the head of the Philistine as a trophy, and put his armor in his tent.

Let us live alone with God. The weakest man who knows God is strong to do exploits. All the might of God awaits the disposal of our faith. As a child by touching a button may set in motion a mighty steamship, making it glide like a swan into her native element, so a stripling who has learned to reckon on God may bring the whole forces of Deity to bear on men and things on the world's battlefield. This is the victory that overcomes the world, the flesh, and the devil—even our faith.

VII

Jonathan

(1 Samuel xviii. 1.)

" Souls that carry on a blest exchange
　Of joys they meet with in their heavenly range,
　And with a fearless confidence make known
　The sorrows sympathy esteems its own,
　Daily derive increasing light and force
　From such communion in their pleasant course;
　Feel less the journey's roughness and its length;
　Meet their opposers with united strength;
　And one in heart, in interest and design,
　Gird up each other to the race divine."

COWPER.

IN heaven's vault there are what are known as binary
stars, each probably a sun, with its attendant train of
worlds, revolving around a common center, but blending
their rays so that they reach the watcher's eye as one clear
beam of light. So do twin souls find the center of their
orbit in each other; and there is nothing in the annals of
human affection nobler than the bond of such a love between two pure, high-minded, and noble men, whose love
passes that of women. Such love was celebrated in ancient
classic story, and has made the names of Damon and
Pythias proverbial. It has also enriched the literature of
modern days in the love of a Hallam and a Tennyson.
But nowhere is it more fragrant than on the pages that
contain the memorials of the love of Jonathan and David.

David was in all probability profoundly influenced by the character of Jonathan, who must have been considerably older than himself. It seems to have been love at first sight. "When David had made an end of speaking unto Saul, the soul of Jonathan was knit with the soul of David, and Jonathan loved him as his own soul." He did not, however, avow it on the spot; but that night, as the young shepherd was sitting amid a group of soldiers, recounting with them the events of the memorable day, a royal messenger may have summoned him to Jonathan's pavilion, on entering which he was amazed to be greeted with the warm embrace of a brotherly affection which was never to wane. He had lost Eliab in the morning; but at nightfall he had won a friend that would stick closer than a brother. The boy soldier must have shrunk back as unworthy; he must have ruefully looked down at his poor apparel as unbefitting a royal alliance. But all such considerations were swept away before the impetuous rush of Jonathan's affection, as he stripped himself of robe and apparel, of sword and bow and girdle, and gave them all to David. "Then Jonathan and David made a covenant, because he loved him as his own soul."

I. Consider the Qualities of this Friend whom Jehovah chose for the molding of the character of his beloved, and then be prepared to surrender to his care the choice of your most intimate associates. He knows what your temperament needs, and where to find the companion who shall strengthen you when weak, and develop latent unknown qualities.

He was every inch a man. In true friendship there must be a similarity of tastes and interests. The prime condition of two men walking together is that they should be agreed. And the bond of a common manliness knit these twin souls from the first. Jonathan was every inch a man; as dexterous with the bow as his friend with his sling. Able to flash with indignation, strong to bear without quailing the brunt of his father's wrath, fearless to espouse the cause of his friends at whatever cost, he was capable of inspiring a single armor-bearer with his own ardent spirit of attacking an army; of turning the tide of invasion; and of securing the admiration and affection of the entire people, who, standing between him and his father, refused to let him die. When Jonathan fell on Gilboa it was no fulsome flattery that led his friend, in his pathetic elegy, to exclaim:

> "Thy glory, O Israel, is slain upon thy high places!
> How are the mighty fallen!"

He was withal very sensitive and tender. It is the fashion in some quarters to emphasize the qualities supposed to be specially characteristic of men—those of strength, courage, endurance—to the undervaluing of the tenderer graces more often associated with women. But in every true man there must be a touch of woman, as there was in the ideal Man, the Lord Jesus. In him there is neither male nor female, because there is the symmetrical blending of both; and in us, too, there should be strength and sweetness, courage and sympathy; the oak and the vine, the rock and the moss that covers it with its soft green mantle.

Jonathan had a marvelous power of affection. He loved David as himself; he was prepared to surrender without a pang his succession to his father's throne, if only he might be next to his friend; his was the love that expresses itself in tender embraces and tears, that must have response from the object of its choice.

> "I am distressed for thee, my brother Jonathan!
> Very pleasant hast thou been unto me:
> Thy love to me was wonderful,
> Passing the love of women."

We judge a man by his friends, and the admiration he excites in them. Any man whom David loved must have been possessed of many of those traits so conspicuous in David himself. Much is said of the union of opposites, and it is well when one is rich where the other is poor; but the deepest love must be between those whose natures are close akin. As we, therefore, review the love that united these two, now forever joined in the indissoluble bonds of eternity, we must attribute to Jonathan the poetic sensitiveness, the tender emotion, the heroism of that courage, the capacity for those uprisings of the soul to all that was pure and lovely and noble, which were so conspicuous in David.

He was distinctly religious. When first introduced to us, as, accompanied by his armor-bearer, he climbs single-handed to attack the Philistine garrison, strongly intrenched behind rocky crags, he speaks as one familiar with the ways of God, to whom there is no restraint "to save by many or by few"; and when the appointed sign is given it is accepted as a presage of the victory which the Lord is about to give (1 Sam. xiv.).

As he stands beside his father on the hillside, and sees the stripling descend to slay Goliath and win a great victory for Israel, he discerns the hand of the Lord working a great victory for Israel, and his soul lifts itself in holy thought and thanksgiving (1 Sam. xix. 5).

When the two friends are about to be torn from each other, with little hope of renewing their blessed intercourse, Jonathan finds solace in the fact of the divine appointment, and the Lord being between them. Between them, not in the sense of division, but of connection; as the ocean unites us with distant lands, whose shores she laves, whose freights she bears to our wharves. However far we are parted from those we love, we are intimately near in God, whose presence infills and inwraps us; thus streams mingle in the ocean to which they pour tributary tides.

And when, in the last interview the friends ever had, they met by some secret arrangement in a wood, "Jonathan came to David there, and strengthened his hand in God." All that those words imply it is not easy to write; our hearts interpret the words, and imagine the stream of holy encouragement that poured from that noble spirit into the heart of his friend. He must be strong who would strengthen another; he must have God, and be in God, who would give the consolations of God to his brother; and we can easily understand how the anguish of Jonathan's soul, torn between filial devotion to his father and his love to his friend, must have driven him back on those resources of the divine nature which are the only solace of men whose lives have been cast in the same fiery crucible.

II. CONSIDER THE CONFLICT OF JONATHAN'S LIFE.—He was devoted to his father. He was always found associated with that strange dark character, melancholy to madness, the prey of evil spirits, and yet so keenly susceptible to music, and so quick to respond to the appeal of chivalry, patriotism, and generous feeling; resembling some mountain lake, alternately mirroring mountains and skies, and swept by dark storms. Father and son were together in life, as they were "undivided in death."

When his father first ascended the throne of Israel the Lord was with him, and Jonathan knew it (1 Sam. xx. 13). It must have been an exceeding delight to him to feel that the claims of the father were identical with the claims of God, and the heart of the young man must have leaped up in a blended loyalty to both. But the fair prospect was soon overcast. The Lord departed from Saul; and immediately his power to hold the kingdom waned, the Philistines invaded his land, his weapons of defense failed him, his people followed him trembling, and Samuel told him that his kingdom could not continue. Then followed that dark day when Saul intruded on the priestly office in offering sacrifice. The ominous sentence was spoken: "The Lord hath sought him a man after his own heart, and the Lord hath appointed him prince unto his own people."

From that moment Saul's course was always downward; but Jonathan clung to him as if he hoped that by his own allegiance to God he might reverse the effects of his father's failure and still hold the kingdom for their race.

At first this was not so difficult. There was no one to divide his heart with his father; it was not, therefore, a hardship for him to imperil his life in unequal conflict with the Philistines; and his heart must have been fired with the gladdest anticipations as, through the woods where honey dropped, he pursued the Philistines, with all Israel at his heel, smiting them from Michmash to Aijalon. His hopes, however, were destined to disappointment; for, instead of the revival which he had pictured to himself, he saw his father drifting further down the strong tide that bore him out from God. Saul's failure in the matter of the destruction of the Amalekites, the dark spirit which possessed and terrified him, the alienation of Samuel—these things acted as a moral paralysis on that brave and eager heart. What could he do to reverse the decisions of that fated soul; how stem the torrent; how turn the enemy from the gate? Surely it was this hopelessness of being able to alter any of these things that made him unable to meet Goliath. Many a time, as he heard the terrible roar of the giant's challenge, he must have felt the uprisings of a noble impulse to meet him, slay him, or die. But there came over his soul the blight of despair. What could he do when the destiny of the land he loved seemed already settled?

When he woke up to find how truly he loved David, a new difficulty entered his life. Not outwardly, because, though Saul eyed David with jealousy, there was no open rupture. David went in and out of the palace, was in a position of trust, and was constantly at hand for the intercourse for which each yearned. But when the flames of hostility, long smoldering in Saul's heart, broke forth, the true anguish of his life began. On the one hand, his duty as son and subject held him to his father, though he knew his father was doomed, and that union with him meant disaster to himself ; on the other hand, all his heart cried out for David.

His love for David made him eager to promote reconciliation between his father and his friend. It was only when repeated failure had proved the fruitlessness of his dream that he abandoned it; and then the thought must have suggested itself to him: Why not extricate yourself from this sinking ship while there is time? Why not join your fortunes with his whom God hath chosen ? The new fair kingdom of the future is growing up around him—identify yourself with it, though it be against your father.

The temptation was specious and masterful, but it fell blunt and ineffectual at his feet. Stronger than the ties of human love were those of duty, sonship, loyalty to God's anointed king; and in some supreme moment he turned his back on the appeal of his heart, and elected to stand beside his father. From that choice he never flinched. When David departed whither he would, Jonathan went back to the city. His father might sneer at his league with the son of Jesse, but he held his peace ; and when finally Saul started for his last battle with the Philistines, Jonathan fought beside him, though he knew that David was somehow involved in alliance with them.

It was one of the grandest exhibitions of the triumph of

principle over passion, of duty over inclination, that the annals of history record.   Jonathan died as a hero; not only
because of his prowess in battle with his country's foes,
but because of his victory over the strongest passion of the
human heart, the love of a strong man, in which were
blended the strands of a common religion, a common enthusiasm for all that was good and right.

Conflicts like these await us all—when the appointment
of God says one thing and the choice of the heart says
another; when the wind sets in from one quarter and the
tide from the opposite one.   Whenever this befalls thee,
may God's grace enable thee to follow as straight a course,
as true to the loftiest dictates of conscience, as Jonathan,
the son of Saul!

VIII

Outside the House, and In

(Psalm lix. 9, 17.)

" Unholy phantoms from the deep arise,
    And gather through the gloom before mine eyes;
    But all shall vanish at the dawning ray—
    When the day breaks the shadows flee away.

" He maketh all things good unto his own,
    For them in every darkness light is strown;
    He will make good the gloom of this my day—
    Till that day break and shadows flee away."
                S. J. Stone.

IN the Hebrew the difference between the words *wait* and *sing*, as appearing in this passage, is very slight. They are spelled, indeed, alike, with the exception of a single letter. The parallelism, therefore, between these two verses is very marked.

    9. " Upon thee, O my Strength, I will wait:
        For God is my high tower."

    17. " Unto thee, O my Strength, I will sing:
        For God is my high tower."

The inscription indicates the occasion on which this psalm —one of the oldest—was written: "A Psalm of David, when Saul sent, and they watched the house to kill him." The allusions of the psalm substantiate this title, especially

that of the sixth and fourteenth verses, in which the psalmist compares the troop of soldiers, bitten with their master's
spleen, who encamped around his house, belching out their
curses and threats, to the vicious curs of an Eastern city,
that prowl the streets by day and night, clearing them of
their offal and refuse, and filling the night with their uproar.

> " They return at evening: they make a noise like a dog,
> And go round about the city:
> Behold, they belch out with their mouth."

But meanwhile David is in his house, waiting upon God,
and singing aloud of his mercy in the morning.

I. THE EVENTS WHICH LED UP TO THIS ASSAULT ON
DAVID'S HOUSE.—As the victorious army returned home
from the valley of Elah, the whole land went forth in
greeting. The reapers stayed their labors in the field; and
the vineyards were depleted of the women that plucked the
grapes and the men that trod them in the presses. From
village to town the contagious enthusiasm spread; and the
women came forth out of all the cities of Israel, with song
and dance, with timbrels and tabrets, to meet King Saul.
To the song of victory there came this refrain, which was
strikingly discordant to the soul of the king:

> " Saul hath slain his thousands,
> And David his ten thousands."

In that hour the first jealous thought awoke in Saul's
heart; the pitted speck became visible in the goodly fruit
of his character, which was destined to rot and ruin all.
Happy had he been if he had trodden the hell-spark beneath his feet, or extinguished it in seas of prayer. But
he nursed it till, to change the simile, the trickling stream
undermined the sea-wall and became a raging, turbid flood.

" Saul was very wroth, and the saying displeased him. And he eyed David from that day and forward."

But Saul was more than jealous. He deliberately set himself to thwart God's purpose. Samuel had distinctly told him that the Lord had rent the kingdom of Israel from him, and had given it to a neighbor of his that was better than himself. And, without doubt, as he saw the stripling return with Goliath's head in his hand, and as he heard the song of the Israelite women, the dread certainty suggested itself to him that this was the divinely designated king. "What though he be?" said Saul to himself, as Herod in after days. "I am king, and will see to it that this prediction, at least, shall not come true. A dead man cannot reign; and there are many ways short of direct murder by which a man's life can be taken. But this is what it must come to." He supposed that if only he could take David's life, God's purpose would miscarry and Samuel's predictions be falsified. He is not the last man that has descended into the arena to match himself with God and been crushed in the attempt. No student of history is likely to forget the cry of Julian the Apostate, which mirrors the experience of thousands more: "Thou hast conquered, O Galilean!"

Saul's murderous passion sought to fulfil itself in many ways. On the following day, as David essayed to soothe him with his harp, he twice hurled his javelin at the minstrel, in the hope that if it pinned him to the wall the act might be imputed to insanity. But on each occasion the weapon sped harmlessly past, to quiver in the wall behind, instead of in that young heart.

Next Saul gave him an important military commission, and made him his captain over a thousand, in the vain hope that this sudden elevation into the slippery place of worldly prominence and power might turn his head dizzy, and lead him to some traitorous deed, for which death would be the

obvious penalty.   But David behaved himself wisely in all
his ways, avoiding every pitfall, eluding every snare; so that
the king, who watched closely for his falling, became more
than ever convinced that he was God's ward, and stood in
awe of him.

Then he offered the young soldier the hand of his eldest
daughter in marriage, and treacherously withdrew the offer
as the time of the nuptials approached—the intention being
to arouse his ardent spirit to retaliate, and so to become
liable to the charge of treason.   But all his efforts failed to
arouse even a transient impulse for revenge.

Again, by the lure of his second daughter, Michal, as prize
to be won by the evidence of one hundred Philistines having been slain, he sought to involve his rival in frays out of
which only a miracle could bring him unhurt.   But David
returned unscathed with double the number required; and
the love of the people grew.

Thwarted thus far, the God-forsaken monarch, driven by
the awful fury of his jealousy, spake to Jonathan and to all
his servants that they should rid him of David's torment-
ing presence.   But of course this plot failed; for Jonathan
delighted much in David, while all Israel and Judah loved
him, for he went out and came in before them.   Jonathan,
indeed, stood in the breach to turn away his father's anger,
and elicited from him the promise that his friend should
not be put to death.   But his pleadings and reasonings had
only a temporary effect; for shortly after, as the young minstrel endeavored to charm away the spirit of melancholy,
the javelin again quivered past him from the royal hand,
and would have transfixed him to the wall but for his lithe
agility.   It was the evening, and David fled to his young
wife and home.   And Saul, intent on murder, "sent messengers unto David's house, to watch him, and to slay him

in the morning." These were the men whom he characterized so vividly, as we have seen.

Michal's quick wit saved her husband's life. She let
him down through the window, and he went and escaped;
while an image, covered with a quilt and placed in the bed,
led Saul's emissaries to suppose that he was sick. There
was no real occasion, however, for her to resort to either
teraphim or deceit to secure his safety from her father's
murderous rage; for when, shortly after, the king proposed
to snatch his prey from the midst of the sacred college and
from the very presence of Samuel, three sets of messengers
were rendered powerless by the divine afflatus, and an arrest was put on Saul himself, who was prostrated before the
mighty impression of God's Spirit, and lay helpless on the
earth (1 Sam. xix. 24).

That must have been a marvelous experience for David.
To the eye of sense there was absolutely nothing to prevent
the king's messengers, or the king himself, from taking
him. But by faith he knew that he was being kept within
the curtains of an impalpable pavilion, and that he was hidden beneath an invisible wing. As the air, itself invisible,
fills the diving-bell and saves the inmates from the inrush-
ing water; as a stream of electricity poured over a heap
of jewels protects them from the hand of the plunderer;
as the raying forth of Christ's majesty flung his captors to
the ground, so did the presence of God environ and protect both Samuel and David. And thus our God will still
do for each of his persecuted ones.

> " In the secret of his tabernacle shall he hide them ;
> He shall set them up upon a rock."

II. David's Composure amid the Assaults of his
Foes.—This hunted man is a lesson for men and angels.

Saul is his inveterate foe; traps and snares are laid for him
on all sides. Sometimes the sun shines on his golden locks,
but more often the skies are thick with cloud and storm.
Now the women of Israel welcome him; and again he is
torn from his wife, and driven forth from his home to go
whither he may. Yet all the while his heart is tranquil and
reposeful; yea, it actually breaks forth into praise, as the
closing verses of this psalm prove. What was the secret of
his serenity?

It lay, first, in the conviction of what God was. God
was *his strength*—that was God within him; God was *his
high tower*—that was God without and around him. He
was God-possessed and God-encompassed. God dwelt in
him and he in God; there was no demand for which he
was not sufficient, no peril which he could not keep at bay.
What a blessed conception is here! You are too weak for
some great task which has been intrusted to your care. In
your judgment it would task the energies of the best and
wisest you know; but lo! it has been placed in your hands.
"O Lord," you cry, "wherewith shall I save Israel? Behold, my family is the poorest in Manasseh; and I am the
least in my father's house." Then the Spirit of God reveals
God as strength, that he may be so received into the heart
as to become the principle of a new and heaven-born energy, which shall rise superior to every difficulty, and breast
the mightiest waves that would beat the swimmer back.
Listen to the laughter of the Apostle's soul as he surveys
herculean tasks on the one hand and enormous opposing
obstacles on the other, and says with unhesitating assurance,
"I can do all things through Christ that strengtheneth me."
O weakest of the weak, remember Jesus Christ, and take
him to be the strength of thy life; be strong, yea, be strong,
in the grace that is in Christ Jesus.

Or turn to the other conception. See those fugitive sol·

diers, hotly pursued by their enemies as clouds before the
Biscay gale.   On yonder cliff is perched a fortress, whose
mighty walls and towers, if only they can be reached, will
insure protection.   Breathlessly they scale the ascent, rush
across the drawbridge, let down the portcullis, and fling
themselves on the sward, and know that they are safe.
God is all that to the soul which has learned to put him
between itself and everything.   We have not even to flee
to God, for that implies that we have been allured out of
him; but we are to abide in him; to stand fast in the liberty wherewith he has made us free; to reckon that, whatever Satan may say and however he may rage, we are absolutely secure so long as we abide in God.

When we realize these things, and add the further conception with which the psalm closes, that God is the fount
of mercy; when we dare to believe that there is mercy in
Saul's hate, mercy in the difficulties of our lot, mercy in the
clouds that veil our sky and the flints that line our path,
mercy in the sharpest, bitterest experiences, then we can
sing, we can say with David:

" I will sing of thy strength;
  Yea, I will sing aloud of thy mercy in the morning:
  For thou hast been my high tower, and a refuge in the day of my
    distress."

It lay, next, in his attitude toward God: " O my Strength,
I will *wait* on thee."   The word so translated is used in the
Hebrew of the shepherd watching his flock, of the watch-
man on the tower, of the sentry passing to and fro upon
his beat.   Is this our habitual attitude?   Too many direct
their prayer, but do not look up the ladder for the descending angels, laden with the heavenly answer.   Many a ship
passes in the night, touching at our wharf with the precious
freight which we have been praying for; but we are not

there to receive it.   Many a relieving force comes up the pass with glittering spears and flashing helmets; but our gates are closed.   Many a dove comes to our window from the weltering waste of waters ; but we are too immersed in other things to notice its light tap.   We pray, but we do not wait; we ask, but we do not expect to receive; we knock, but we are gone before the door is opened.

This lesson is for us to learn—to reckon on God ; to tarry for the vision; to wait till Samuel comes; to believe that he who taught us to trust cannot deceive our trust; to be sure that none of them that wait on him can be ashamed ; to appropriate by faith ; and to know that we have the petitions we desired ; nay, to do more, to take them and count them ours, though we have no responsive emotion, no sense of possession.   This is waiting upon God; this will keep us calm and still, though dreaded evils frown around our homestead; this will change our waiting into song.

IX

ᛋᚺᚲ Message of the Arrows

(I SAMUEL xx. 21–37.)

Toils and foes assailing, friends quailing, hearts failing,
　　　Shall threat in vain:
If he be providing, presiding, and guiding
　　　To him again."

J. M. NEALE.

JONATHAN had considerable influence with his father.
Saul did nothing, either great or small, which he did not
"uncover to his ear." For his love's sake, as well as for
his father's, he was extremely eager to effect a reconciliation between him to whom he owed the allegiance of son
and subject and this fair shepherd-minstrel-warrior, who had
so recently cast a sunny gleam upon his life. In all probability Jonathan was much David's senior; but in his pure
and noble breast the fountain of love rose unquenched by
years. On more than one occasion he had communed with
his father concerning his friend, so far impressing Saul as
to make him swear that David should not be put to death.
Thus when David returned in hot haste from Naioth, leaving Saul under the spell of prophecy, and asked him what
he had done to arouse such inveterate hate, asserting that
there was but a step between him and death, Jonathan did
not hesitate to assure him of his willingness to do whatever
his soul desired.

It was the eve of the feast of the new moon, when Saul invited the chief men of his kingdom to a banquet; and the friends agreed that this was an opportune moment for testing the real sentiments of Saul.   David suggested that he should absent himself from the royal banquet, visiting his father's home at Bethlehem instead.   It would be quite easy for him to do this and yet be back by the third day. In the meantime Jonathan was to watch narrowly his father's behavior, and mark his tone, noting whether it was rough or kind.

The general outline of this scheme was arranged within the palace; but there were confidences to be exchanged so intimate, words to be said so tender, a covenant to be entered into so pathetic, a means of communication to be arranged so secret, that it seemed wiser to continue the conversation in some secluded spot, where only the living things of the woods, that can tell no tales, could behold the flowing tears and hear the outbreak of those manly sobs that could not be choked down.   There was indeed one other witness; for Jonathan was a deeply religious man.   It was his habit to live in the presence of the God of Israel; and to him he made his appeal as he bared his heart to his friend, entreating him to deal truly with him, and pleading that in that certain future, when God had cut off David's enemies from the earth, he would not forget the claims of friendship and cut off his kindness from his house.

Surely the fateful field of Gilboa was already casting a premonitory shadow over Jonathan's heart; and he felt the time would come when David would exercise supreme power, and might be tempted to stamp out the possibility of rivalry on the part of Jonathan's heirs by exterminating the royal house.   In his anxiety he made him swear again, and afterward proposed the ingenious and significant plan in which his art and directions to the little lad would express by a swift telegraphy the secret which would either lift David to peace and safety or thrust him into the depths of despair.

It is impossible to read the story without thinking of the boys that carry the buff-colored envelopes, so little conscious of what the messages may mean to those in whose hands they place them, here filling them with ecstasy and there with bitter anguish. The arrows are flying still; the little lads are fulfilling their unconscious ministries with respect to them. Often they fall short of the mark, then again they fly beyond it. How often they are beyond! O strong arm, why shoot them with so much energy? O wind, why carry them so lightly? Hearts are breaking as the bow-string twangs. Lives take their color of light or shadow ever after, just because of a few yards less or more!

I. THE ARROWS TAUGHT THAT A STRONG AND NOBLE FRIEND WAS STANDING IN THE BREACH.—Jonathan was a jewel of the first water: unequaled in his use of arms, daring to recklessness on the field of battle, swifter than the eagle, stronger than the lion, yet tender as a woman; true to his friend; so capable of inspiring attachment that his armor-bearer would face an army at his side; so tenacious of his principles that he clung to his father's fallen fortunes even though he had suffered from that father all that jealousy could suggest of bitter insult and murderous hate.

It was no child's play that he undertook in the sacred name of friendship; and probably he was quite prepared for the outburst that followed his manly protest for his absent friend. On the first feast-day Saul noticed David's absence, but said nothing; on the second, however, when his seat was still vacant, he turned sharply on his son Jonathan and asked the reason: "Why cometh not the son of Jesse to meat, neither yesterday, nor to-day?" Jonathan

instantly made the preconcerted answer about David's desire to see his family, and made out that he had himself
given permission for his absence.   This identification of
himself with David brought on Jonathan an outburst of ungovernable rage.   Saul's fury knew no bounds.   With stinging allusion to Jonathan's mother, his own wife, as the source
of his son's perversity; with taunts that were intended to
instil into Jonathan's heart the poison which was working
in his own; with demands that David should be instantly
fetched and put to death, the monarch clearly showed his
inveterate hatred and determination that the son of Jesse
should no longer tarry above-ground.   Jonathan made one
vain attempt to reason with the furious monarch; he might
as well have tried to arrest the swelling of Jordan in the
time of flood.   In a paroxysm of ungovernable passion the
king cast his spear at him to smite him.   Then Jonathan
knew that they must prepare for the worst, and left the
table in fierce anger, being grieved for his friend, because
his father had done him shame.

Never be ashamed to own a friend.   Do not count him
your friend whose name you are ashamed to mention, and
with whose lot you blush to be identified; but when you
have entered into an alliance with another soul, whom you
love as Jonathan loved David, dare to stand up for him at
all cost to your comfort and relations with those who do
not know your friend as you know him.   "To be obscure,
and poor, and out of court favor"—that is the greater reason why you should take his part.   It is a noble thing when
a man or woman in some gay and frivolous circle, where
fashion and pride rule, dares to take the part of some un-
popular righteous cause, of some maligned but holy servant
of God, of some unpolished but sterling associate.   This
stamps the confessor with the guinea-die of native worth.

It is easier to storm a fort than to withstand the covert sneer, the contemptuous look.

But there is something still nobler—when one dares in any company to avow his loyalty to the Lord Jesus. Like David, he is now in obscurity and disrepute; his name is not popular; his gospel is misrepresented; his followers are subjected to rebuke and scorn. These are days when to stand up for anything more than mere conventional religion must cost something; and for this very reason let us never flinch, but as we trust that he will confess our name before his Father and the angels, let us not be ashamed of his. Jonathan's arrows showed that he did not hesitate to stand alone for David; let our words assure Him, who is just now hidden, that we will bear scorn, obloquy, and death for his dear name.

Never be ashamed to speak up for the cause of truth. How often the spirit of expediency whispers in our ear, " Let it pass; wait till the dinner is done; do not make a gazing-stock of yourself; take an opportunity of private remonstrance; sit still; be pleasant; we will see what can be done presently"! Jonathan took the nobler course. The dainties were on his plate, but he would not touch them; the cup was in his hand, but he would not place it to his lips; his father was before him, with his claims on his reverence and respect—the king, with the power of life and death in his mouth; but he dared not hold his peace. Had it been simply a question of his own position or respect, of mere politeness, civility, courtesy due to age, he would have been the first to put his hand upon his mouth and be silent. But it was a question of truth, righteousness, justice; and if he were to be still, the very stones in the wall would cry out against him, and he would forfeit the respect of his own conscience.

But it may be asked, Is it not unseemly to obtrude
opinions among those who are older and more learned
than ourselves? Yes; but there is all the difference in the
world between opinions spun like cobwebs from the brain,
or caught up at second-hand, and those great basic principles of truth, morality, and right which are witnessed to by
conscience. And when you stand up for these, you do not
seek to exalt your own goodness or win an advantage, but
simply to lift the standard from being trampled in the mud.
Let the arrows witness to the simplicity and fervor of your
allegiance to whatever is lovely and of good report.

II. The Arrows Spoke of Imminent Danger. — "Jonathan knew that it was determined of his father to put David
to death." As the lad ran, Jonathan shot an arrow beyond
him. "And as soon as the lad was gone, David arose out
of a place toward the south, and fell on his face to the
ground, and bowed himself three times: and they kissed
one another, and wept one with another, until David ex-
ceeded." There was no need for Jonathan to enter into
explanations. David knew that "the Lord had sent him
away" (verse 22).

"The arrows are beyond thee." You have hoped against
hope; you have tried to keep your position; you have done
your duty, pleaded your cause, sought the intercession of
your friends, prayed, wept, agonized. But it is all in vain;
the arrows' flight proves that you must go whither you
may. Behind you is the sunny morning, before you a
lowering sky; behind you the blessed enjoyment of friendship, wife, home, royal favor, and popular adulation, before
you an outcast's life. The heart clings to the familiar and
beloved. But the message of those arrows cannot be resisted. There is no alternative but to tear yourself away,
take your life in your hand, and go forth, though you

know not whither. But take these thoughts for your comfort.

1. *There are things we never leave behind.* David had an inalienable possession in the love of his friend, in the devotion of the people, in the memory of God's goodness, in his experience of his delivering care, in the sense of the divine presence which was ever beside him, in the psalms which he had already made for himself, as well as for the world. There are threads woven into the fabric of our life which can never be extracted or obliterated.

2. *There is a divine purpose determining our course.* To the lad there was but royal caprice in the flight of the arrows. "What are you doing, my little fellow?" "I am picking up the prince's arrows; we generally go for game, but he is playing at it to-day." That was all he knew. How little did he divine the purpose of his master, and still less realize that each flitting arrow was, so to speak, taken from God's quiver and directed by his hand! There is no chance in a good man's life. Let us recognize the providence of the trifle. Let us believe that behind the arrows' flight there is the loving purpose of our Heavenly Father. *He* is sending us away.

3. *The going forth is necessary to secure greater happiness than we leave.* Had David lingered in the palace, his life would have been forfeited, and he would have missed all the glory and bliss with which his cup ran over in after years. This was the way to the throne. Only thus could the sentence whispered in his ear by Samuel years before be realized. This mountain-pass, with its jagged flints, was the path to the happy valley. The nest was stirred up that he might acquire powers of flight; the precious wine of his life was emptied from vessel to vessel to lose its strong flavor of must; the trellis-work was taken down that the plant might stand alone.

Follow the arrows' flight, then—beyond the warm circle
in which you have so long been sheltered; beyond the
southland to the icy north; beyond the known to the unknown. Like another Abraham, go into the land which
God will show thee; like another Columbus, turn thy prow
in the wake of the setting sun. Let David's assurance be
yours:

> "Thou wilt not leave my soul in Hades,
>   Neither wilt thou suffer thine Holy One to see corruption:
>   Thou wilt show me the path of life."

III. The Arrows Taught that Human Love must
Suffer Separation.—This was the last meeting of these
two noble hearts for a long time. Indeed, the friends only
met once more, shortly before Jonathan's death. They had
realized that this must be so. The soul of Jonathan, especially, seems to have been overcast with the impression
that their happy intercourse would never again be renewed;
therefore he pledged David with that pathetic vow to be
faithful to his seed, and to remember their love when all
his enemies had been cut off. "Go in peace," Jonathan
said, finally, as though he could no longer bear the awful
anguish of that parting, "forasmuch as we have sworn
both of us in the name of the Lord, saying, The Lord
be between me and thee, and between my seed and thy
seed forever." Then David arose and departed, to become a fugitive and an outlaw, liable at any moment
to capture and violent death; while Jonathan returned
thoughtfully and sadly to the palace, where he must spend
the rest of his life in contact with one who had no sympathy for his noble sentiments, who had outraged his tenderest sensibilities.

These are the hours that leave scars on hearts and
whiten the hair. The world in its rush is so unconscious

of all the tragedies which are taking place around. Young hearts suffer till they can suffer no more; aged ones cannot forget; and years after some scene like this, eyes will fill with tears as it is recalled. But Christ comes to us in these dark moments, as of old to the disciples, on whom had broken the full import of their Master's approaching departure. "Let not your heart be troubled: . . . trust in me." There is no comfort like this. To believe that he is ordering each detail; to know that love is prompting each action of his hand, each thought of his mind; to lie back on his bosom and utterly trust him—there is nothing like this to bridge the yawning gulf of separation, with its turbid, rushing stream beneath.

X

Almost Gone

(1 Samuel xxi.; Psalm lvi.)

"But oh, whatever of worst ill betide,
  Choose not this manner to evade your woe:
Be true to God; on him in faith abide,
  And sure deliverance you at length shall know.
  It may be that some path his hand will show
To your dear earthly homes; or he will shape
For you at length a way of glad escape."

Trench.

IT is not easy to walk with God. The air that beats around the Himalaya heights of divine fellowship is rare and hard to breathe; human feet tire after a little; and faith, hard put to it, is inclined to give up the effort of keeping step with the divine pace. So David found it; and there came in his experience a terrible lapse, the steps and consequences of which, together with his recovery, must engage us for a space.

I. The Steps of David's Declension.—The *first* sign of what was impending was his remark to Jonathan that there was but a step between himself and death (1 Sam. xx. 3). Evidently his faith was beginning to falter; for nothing could have been more definite than the divine assurances that he was to be king. He looked at God through the mist of circumstances, which certainly, to the eye of sense, were sufficiently threatening, instead of looking at circumstances through the golden haze of God's very present help. The winds and waves were more daunting than the promise of God was inspiring. The javelin of Saul intercepted the remembrance of the hour, now rapidly receding into the distance, when he had received the anointing oil at the hand of Samuel. The Apostle John says that it is not enough to receive the anointing once; it must *abide* on us; and this was characteristic of our Lord, that the baptism saw the Spirit descending and *abiding upon* him. But perchance David relied too absolutely on what he had received, and neglected the daily renewal of the heavenly unction (John i. 33, 34; 1 John iii. 24).

Next he adopted a subterfuge which was not worthy of him, nor of his great and mighty Friend. This was a further descent from the high place of heavenly fellowship and testimony. God is light, and light is truth; and those who walk with him must put off the works of darkness, and put on the armor of light, walking as children of the day.

Late in the afternoon of the day preceding the weekly Sabbath the king's son-in-law arrived, with a mere handful of followers, at the little town of Nob, situated among the hills about five miles to the south of Gibeah. It was a peaceful, secluded spot, apart from the highways of commerce and war, as became the character and calling of its inhabitants, who were engaged in the service of the sanctuary. Fourscore and six persons that wore the linen ephod dwelt there with their wives, their children and sucklings, their oxen, asses, and sheep. Into the tranquil course of existence in that holy and retired spot hardly a ripple came from the storms that swept the outer world. There was at least no provision made to repel invading footsteps; for no weapon was found there but the sword of Goliath, deposited years before as a trophy by the youthful champion. Probably the great annual convocations had fallen into disuse, and the path to the simple sanctuary was only trodden by occasional visitors, such as Doeg, who came to pay their vows or be cleansed from ceremonial pollution. There was evidently no attempt made to prepare for large numbers; the hard fare of the priests only just sufficed for them, and the presence of two or three additional strangers completely overbalanced the slender supply; there were not five loaves of common bread to spare.

It was necessary to answer the questions and allay the suspicions of the priest; and David did this by pleading the urgency of the mission on which his royal master had sent him. He led Ahimelech to suppose that his young attendants and himself had been at least three days on this expedition; that the king had specially insisted on privacy and secrecy; and that a large escort awaited him at a distance. But a chill struck to his heart while making these excuses to the simple-minded priest, and enlisting his willing coöperation in the matter of provisions and arms, as he saw the dark visage of Doeg, the Edomite, "the chiefest of the herdmen that belonged to Saul." He knew that the whole story would be mercilessly retailed to the vindictive and vengeful monarch. Uneasiness for his unsuspecting host and fear for himself filled his heart; and as soon as the Sabbath was over he left the spot, and with all haste struck across the hills in a southwesterly direction until he cut the deep depression of the valley of Elah, where he had achieved the great victory of his life. Its aspect was strangely altered, its only tenants then being the wild things of earth and sky. Ten miles beyond lay the proud Philistine city of Gath, which at that time had sent its champion forth in all the pride of his stature and strength. Behind

David had left an implacable foe. What worse fate could await him at Gath than that which threatened him each hour he lingered within the limits of Judah! He therefore resolved to make the plunge, probably hoping that the shepherd lad of years ago would not be recognized in the mature warrior, or that the Philistines would be glad to have his aid in their wars against his countrymen.

Not a little to his dismay, and perhaps on account of Goliath's sword hanging at his belt, he was instantly recognized; and the servants of Achish recalled the refrain which had already awoke the jealousy of Saul. He was instantly regarded with hatred, as having slain his ten thousands. His hands had been imbrued in Philistine blood; his fortunes reared from the dust at the expense of bereaved hearts and homes throughout the Philistine territory. Here, however, was an easy opportunity of avenging all. By some means David became aware of the evil impression at court, and saw the immense peril in which he stood of imprisonment or execution. He saved himself by descending to the unworthy subterfuge of counterfeiting the behavior of a madman, drumming on the leaves of the city gate, and allowing his spittle to fall down upon his beard. His device succeeded; and Achish dismissed him with the humorous remark to his servants that he had already madmen enough around him, and had no need of another. This certainly was one of the least dignified episodes in David's varied life, very unworthy of God's anointed; and the shame was that there would have been no need for it if he had not departed through unbelief from the living God.

II. THE PSALM OF THE SILENT DOVE.—At first sight we are startled with the apparently irreconcilable discrepancy between the scenes we have just described and the Fifty-sixth Psalm, the inscription of which associates it with them.   But there is no reason to doubt the accuracy of that ancient note, which is probably due to David's hand, and is at least as old as the first arrangement of the Psalter, in the days of Solomon.

Closer inspection will reveal many resemblances between the singer's circumstances and his touching words; and we are reminded that beneath much which is unworthy and contemptible there may burn a true devotion, an eager yearning after God, a soul of good amid things evil. The cursory spectator would not have supposed that this dissembling madman were meditating thoughts which were to express for all generations the most implicit faith, the sincerest trust.   But so it was.

The major part of this exquisite psalm consists of two stanzas, which culminate in the same refrain; the remainder is full of hope and praise, an expression of the joy with which the psalmist anticipates walking before God in the light of life.

First Stanza (vs. 1–4).—He turns to God from man; to the divine mercy from the serried ranks of his foes, who, surging around him, threaten to engulf and swallow him up; he counts himself as a lonely dove far from its native woods; his heart trembles and misgives amid the many that fight proudly against him; yet he contrasts fear with faith, arguing with himself as to the baselessness of his dread, and contrasting man's fleshy might with God's supreme power.   Thus he climbs up out of the weltering waves, his feet on a rock, a new song in his mouth, the burden of which is, "I will not be afraid."   O happy soul, who hast learned to take thy stand on God as thy rock and fortress!

Second Stanza (vs. 5–9).—Again he is in the depths.   The returning wave has sucked him back.   His boast changed

to a moan, his challenge to complaint. Never a moment
of intermission from the wrestling of his words; not a glint
of respite from the hostility of their thoughts; not a step
which is not watched by the scrutiny of those who lie in
wait for his soul. He wanders fitfully from shelter to shelter; his tears fall thick and fast; his enemies are numerous
as the hairs of his head. Ah, soul, is this thy voice which
but a moment ago was resonant with praise? Alas for
thee! Yet, as we condole, we hear the voice of faith again
ringing out the positive assurance, " I know that God is for
me," and again the old refrain comes back:

> " In God will I praise his word:
> In the Lord will I praise his word.
> In God have I put my trust:
> I will not be afraid.
> What can man do unto me ! "

Third Stanza (vs. 10–13).—There is no further relapse.
His heart is fixed, trusting the Lord; the vows of God are
upon his head. He looks back upon the dark abyss into
which his soul had well-nigh gone, and knows that he is
delivered from it forever. As the morning breaks he sees
the mark of his footprints to the edge of the precipice, and
recognizes the divine power and grace which has delivered
his feet from falling. And now, as once again he regains
the sunny uplands, which he had so shamefully renounced
in his flight from Gibeah to Nob, from Nob to Gath, from
Gath to feigned insanity, he is sure that henceforth he will
walk before God in the light of life. Truth, purity, joy,
shall be the vesture of his soul.

In the extreme anguish of those hours at Gath, when he
thought that the torch of his life would go out in the dark
waters of Philistine hatred, the backslider had returned to
God, had caught the rope by which to spring from the

abyss into the light, and once again sat, as a child at home, anointed with oil, with a table spread before him in the presence of his enemies.

III. THE CONSEQUENCES TO AHIMELECH.—A child of God may be forgiven and restored, yet the consequences of his sin may involve sufferings to many innocent lives. So it was in this instance. It happened shortly after, when Saul was sitting under the tamarisk-tree in Ramah, with his spear in his hand and his servants around him. He was endeavoring to excite their sympathy by enumerating the supposed wrongs he had suffered at the hand of David, and Doeg took the opportunity of ingratiating himself in the royal favor by narrating what he had seen at Nob. He carefully withheld the unsuspecting innocence and ignorance of the priest, and so told the tale as to make it appear that he and his house were accomplices with David's action, and perhaps bent on helping David to gain supreme power. It was in vain that Ahimelech protested his innocence, enumerated David's services, referred to the many occasions on which David had sought his help, persisted in the avowal of his unconsciousness of the quarrel between Saul and his son-in-law; before night fell the white vesture of the priests was soaked with their blood, and every living thing in the little mountain town was smitten with the edge of the sword. By one ruthless act the entire priestly community was exterminated.

There was but one survivor, for Abiathar escaped, carrying the ephod in his hand; and one day, to his horror, David beheld the disheveled, blood-besmeared form of the priest, as he sped breathless and panic-stricken up the valley of Elah, to find shelter with the outlaw band in the cave of Adullam. We shall hear of him again.

Meanwhile, let children of God beware! Sin is bitter to

the conscience of the sinner and in its consequences upon others. Let us walk circumspectly, watchfully, prayerfully, exercising our consciences repeatedly to see if there be any swerving from the path of strict integrity; lest seeds be scattered beyond recovery, to bear bitter harvests in the lives of those who, through their mysterious union with ourselves, are inextricably involved in the consequences of our deeds.

XI

The Cave of Adullam

(I SAMUEL xxii. ; PSALM xxxiv.)

" For good ye are and bad, and like to coins —
Some true, some light; but every one of you
Stamp'd with the image of the king."

TENNYSON.

LEAVING Gath with a very thankful heart for God's delivering mercy, David hastily recrossed the frontier, and found himself again in the kingdom of Saul. His life, however, was in great jeopardy, and he did not dare to expose himself to the royal jealousy. To return to court was impossible; and he did not care to incur the risk of involving his relatives in his troubles by seeking shelter at Bethlehem. There was apparently no alternative but to adopt the life of a fugitive and wanderer amid the hills of Judah, with which his shepherd life had made him so familiar.

Two miles up the valley of Elah from Gath there is a labyrinth of hills and valleys, deeply honeycombed with caves. One of these, near the ancient Canaanitish city of Adullam, and called after it, afforded David for a considerable period the shelter of which he was in search. It is described as a dark vault, the entrance of which is a low window in the perpendicular face of the cliff; and its position made it possible for him to cross from one country to another, as occasion required. Thither fled his whole

family, dreading, no doubt, the violence of Saul's hatred;
and thither also came every one that was in distress, and
every one that was in debt, and every one that was discontented, and he became captain over them.

We need not now enlarge on David's filial love, which
traversed the entire distance from Adullam to Moab to
secure an asylum for his father and mother, who were
probably too aged to stand the hardships and dangers of
his fugitive life. Suffice it to say that his petition was
readily granted by the king of Moab, perhaps on account
of some pride in the Moabite blood that flowed in the veins
of the young Hebrew warrior. But that double journey,
first to secure the shelter, and then to escort the aged
couple thither, evinces a pleasing trait in David's character.
There was no lack of obedience to the first commandment
with promise. It is, however, with the cave and the more
motley group of his adherents that we have now to do.

I. The Cave and its Lessons.—There can be no
doubt that the Holy Ghost, in the minute narration of
these experiences in David's life, desires us to trace an
analogy between his history and that of the Lord Jesus, in
his present rejection and banishment from the throne of the
world. The parallel is as minute as it is instructive.

A rejected king was on the throne. Though anointed by
Samuel, Saul by disobedience had forfeited his right to
reign, and had, so to speak, nullified the effect of the
sacred unction—as we may do also. The sentence of deposition had been pronounced, and was awaiting execution at the appropriate moment. Similarly, the dark fallen
spirit, Satan, was once an anointed cherub, set on the holy
mountain of God, and perfect in his ways from the day
that he was created till unrighteousness was found in him.
Not improbably he derives the title which our Lord gave

him of "prince of this world" from his original appointment as God's vicegerent and representative; but in his
fall he forfeited his glorious position, and man was created
as his substitute to take his place. "What is man? . . . Thou
madest him to have dominion over the works of thy hands."
That power is not yet exercised by man: "We see not yet
all things put under him;" but it will be in the person of
the Son of man, who is already "crowned with glory and
honor."

In the meanwhile Satan still holds the throne of the world.
He has many a time cast his javelin at the King after God's
own heart. In the temptation and in Gethsemane he would
fain have pinned him to the wall. All through the present
age he has been doing his worst to exterminate the incipient
hidden kingdom of Jesus, though he knows that God has
destined it to take the place of his own. But all his at-
tempts must fail. As Saul fell on the field of Gilboa,
so the prince of darkness shall be finally cast into the
bottomless pit.

David's kingdom was hidden. It was a true kingdom,
though in mystery, veiled in the darkness of Adullam's
cave, and concealed in the labyrinth of valleys and hills.
He had fallen into the ground to die, that he might not
abide alone, but bring forth much fruit. It is a mysterious
process through which the little seed-corn passes in the
winter, when it surrenders itself to the destructive forces
that lie in wait in the red mold and seize on its tender
fabric: "Exposed to wintry winds; trodden under the feet
of those who drive the rake and harrow over it; buried out
of sight and left alone, as if cast out by God and man to
endure the slow process of a daily dissolution; then melted
by rains and heats until its form is marred, and it seems
useless to either God or man." Such was the experience
of David; and it was also the experience of that divine

King who fell into the mystery of forsakenness on the cross, and the mystery of rejection in the grave; and whose person and kingdom are now altogether hidden from the world of men.

The day is not far distant when the Lord, who is hidden until the time of the restitution of all things, shall be manifested with his saints, and take to himself his great power and reign. The pearl which he won from the ocean caves shall be worn on his brow; the treasure for which he bought the field of the world shall be spread forth for the admiration of the universe; the army which he has constituted from such unpromising materials shall follow him on white horses in radiant array. In the meanwhile his kingdom is "in mystery."

David and his followers were in separation. Driven without the camp of Israel, they had no alternative. With the feasts and pageants, the counsels and decisions, the home politics and foreign wars of Saul they had no immediate connection, though the cave of Adullam could not but exert an important indirect influence on the whole realm. The lot of an exile, the path of the wanderer and stranger, were meted out to David and those who were willing to share his lot. His way to the throne lay through multiplied difficulties and sorrows; and although he must have prized the freer air, the sense of liberty, the deliverance from the heartless and godless etiquette of the palace, there must have been a perpetual sadness and loneliness in his soul.

The true King of men is still outside human politics and society. We cannot have him and them. Those who desire to be his subjects, and to share the rewards and glories of those coming days when he shall have dominion from sea to sea, and from the river to the ends of the earth, must go out to him without the camp, willing to forsake all that they have, and be counted the offscouring of all things.

David was content to await God's time.   Whatever provocation Saul gave, he never retaliated.   However easy the opportunity of gaining an advantage over his vindictive pursuer, he never availed himself of it.   He was prepared to wait God's time, and to receive supreme power in God's way.   He quieted himself as a weaned child.   His perpetual refrain is recorded in his own words: " My soul, wait thou only upon God ; for my expectation is from him."   It was as though he sat down in patience and submission till God made his foes the footstool of his feet, and set him as his king on his holy hill of Zion.   It is thus, through these passing centuries, that our Saviour is waiting.   Now is the time of the kingdom and *patience* of Jesus Christ ; here is the patience of the saints ; while the eager expectation and yearning of the whole creation is waiting for the manifestation of the sons of God.   " Ourselves also, which have the first-fruits of the Spirit, even we ourselves groan within ourselves, waiting for our adoption, to wit, the redemption of our body.   For by hope were we saved : but hope that is seen is not hope : for who hopeth for that which he seeth ? But if we hope for that which we see not, then do we with patience wait for it."

II. The Cave and its Inmates.—The tidings of David's return to Judah, and of his retreat in the shelter of the cave, spread swiftly and mysteriously throughout the whole land ; and those who were sorely pressed by misery, poverty, and bitterness of soul began to flock around him. The young leader soon found himself at the head of four hundred men—a very motley crew!   For the few who were loyal to him there were preponderating multitudes who were full of their own grievances and eager only for their redress. The sacred historian says that their faces were like the faces of lions, and that they were as swift as roes upon the mountains; but their tempers were probably turbulent and fierce, requiring all the grace and tact and statesmanship of which the young ruler was capable, to reduce them to discipline and order. It was surely no small feat so to organize such materials that they became the nucleus of the greatest army of their time, and carried the standard of Israel to the fullest limits it ever reached.

We must not think of David at this time of his career as a bandit or freebooter chief; but rather as improvising a frontier guard to defend the land against the Amalekites and Philistines, who were perpetually raiding it at the time of harvest, sweeping away the results of the farmers' toils. Thus he became the benefactor and defender of his people, though exiled from them. In the common talk of the time his men and he were described as a wall to the great sheep-masters and agriculturists of southern Judah, "both by night and day" (1 Sam. xxv. 16).

It is impossible not to turn from David to Him who, though cast out from the scheme of this world and its prince, is ever gathering around his standard the poor and outcast, the leper and sinner, the blind and bruised and broken-hearted, those who are in distress, in debt, and discontented, and making them into soldiers that shall win the world for himself.

Did these wild, rough soldiers find a new center for their life in David? We have found a new object in the Lord Jesus, for whom to live is life indeed, and for whom to die is gain.

Did this new center draw them away from attachment and association with the decadent kingdom of Saul? Our oneness with the living Saviour has made us unworldly by making us *other*worldly. We have cast in our lot with him, and become citizens of the New Jerusalem, and are glad to confess ourselves strangers and pilgrims.

Did they put off the manners and customs of their old life, and allow the shuttle of love and devotion to weave the fabric of a new character? We have put off the old man with his doings, and have put on the new man, which is being renewed unto knowledge after the image of Him that created him.

Did they love David for removing their discontent, alleviating their distress, and relieving them from the disorder and anxiety of their existence? Much more should we love Him who has done more for us than even David did for his poor followers. He has paid our debts with his precious blood; relieved us from our creditors by meeting them himself; clothed us in his perfect beauty; allayed our sorrows; calmed and stilled our souls.

Did the attachment between David and his followers grow with the years, cementing them in a fellowship which was the result of sharing common dangers—the bivouac fire by night, the toilsome march by day, the brush with the foe? What an incentive to us to seek a fellowship with our blessed Lord that shall grow closer for every day of trial we share with him!

III. THE CAVE AND ITS SONG.—Many allusions connect the Thirty-fourth Psalm with the cave of Adullam. It was there that the little host needed the encamping angel; there that the young lions roared, as they ranged the wilds in search of food; there also that God's care was perpetually laid under requisition to keep the bones of the fugitives, lest they should be broken by falling down the crags (vs. 7, 10, 20).

We can imagine the leader, one evening, when the anxieties and fatigues of the day were over, gathering his troop around him with the words, " Come, ye children, hearken unto me, and I will teach you the fear of the Lord." Then, in quick succession, the three exhortations, " O magnify the Lord with me. . . . O taste and see that the Lord is good. . . . O fear the Lord, ye his saints." Then, perhaps, from all their voices came the full chorus, " The Lord redeemeth the soul of his servants: and none of them that trust in him shall be desolate."

The soul which is living a separated life, with sin judged, forsaken, and forgiven behind it, may count on these four:

Deliverance—even in the midst of difficulties and perplexities which have been caused by its own misdeeds (vs. 4, 7, 17, 19).

Enlightenment—for what the dawn is to the weary watcher, that God will be to the soul that has long groped in the dark, if only the face is turned toward his (verse 5).

Perfect provision—so that it shall lack nothing which it really needs (verse 10).

The sense of God's nighness—nearer than the nearest, more real than the presence or absence of any (verse 18).

If, in that cave, with so many things to distract him, compelled to spend every hour in the presence of his men, David was able to realize the presence of God, how much more possible it must be for us! And when once that is realized, all the conditions of the best life are fulfilled.

What makes the difference between the dull and gray of winter and the beauty of the spring? Is it not that the sun is nigh, and nature knows it, and assimilates his glorious color?

So, backslider! broken heart! contrite spirit! do not look back on past failure and shortcoming, nor stand in dread of recurring sin ; but look up and away to the face of Jesus. Do not, I pray you, live on the dying, but on the living side. Dwell in the secret place of the Most High. Abide in the house of the Lord all the days of your life.   Enter with boldness the holiest, to remain there.   Ask the Holy Spirit to enable you to realize the constant presence of God.   Say to yourself many a time each day, even when you do not feel it, "Thou art nigh; thou art here."   Make your home in the sense of God's nearness.   Oh, taste and see the sweetness of such a life.

It was thus that Jesus thought of his Father; and it is thus that you will realize the happiest, strongest experiences possible to the saints.   "The Lord is nigh unto them that are of a broken heart; and saveth such as be of a contrite spirit."

XII

The White Stone

(I Samuel xxiii. 6; Psalm xxvii.)

> "Will not God impart his light
> To them that ask it? Freely—'tis his joy,
> His glory, and his nature, to impart;
> But to the proud, uncandid, insincere,
> Or negligent inquirer, not a spark."
>
> COWPER.

IT is not perfectly clear where David was when he was joined by Abiathar. If we consider the time we are disposed to fix the massacre of the priests shortly after his flight to Gath; and, in that case, Abiathar must have come to him while David was in his first prolonged hiding-place in the cave of Adullam. It is on this supposition that we have already sketched the fugitive coming thither, breathless and disheveled.

If, however, we judge by the position given to the incident on the page of Scripture, we should be disposed to locate it in the forest of Hareth, a tract of country a little to the south of Adullam, and not far from Hebron. The prophet Gad, who had recently joined the young refugee, and was destined to share the fortunes of his long career, living to chronicle his entire history, seems to have advised this exchange. The open country, in the case of pursuit, would be safer than a cave, which might be closed at the entrance and become a death-trap (1 Sam. xxii. 5 ; 1 Chron. xxi. 9 ; xxix. 29).

On the other hand, the verse quoted above suggests that Abiathar came to David at Keilah.   But good authorities question the authenticity of the words "to Keilah," especially as the Septuagint reads : " It came to pass, when Abiathar, son of Ahimelech, fled to David, then he went down with David to Keilah, having the ephod in his hand." If this were so, the inquiries mentioned in the previous verses (1–5) would have been made, as was the custom in those days, through the Urim and Thummim.

There is no need to delay further in the attempt to fix what is of no material importance.   Our present purpose is rather to bring into prominence David's lifelong habit of waiting upon God for direction and guidance.   It is instructive and stimulating to notice that the successive steps of his checkered career were taken after very definite waiting upon God.   It was as though the advice he gives to us all, in the psalm which dates from this period, was the outcome of his own deepest experience and practice :

> " Wait on the Lord :
> Be strong, and let thine heart take courage :
> Yea, wait thou on the Lord."

The expression of the psalmist's soul in the Twenty-seventh Psalm ; his practice, as delineated by the historian ; and the lessons which we may well incorporate into our daily walk—such is the trend of our thought.

I. THE PSALMIST'S ATTITUDE AND DESIRE.—There are several items of internal evidence which connect the Twenty-seventh Psalm with this period of David's life. His fortunes were as dark as the interior of Adullam's cave, therefore he spoke of God as his light; he was in daily peril, therefore it was his comfort that God would be his salvation. Jehovah was more really his stronghold than even that fortress of rock (R.V., marg.). Evil-doers might come on him to eat up his flesh, but they would stumble and fall, as Goliath had done in that very ravine; hosts might encamp against him, but his heart would not fear; war might rise against him, but in this would he be confident. He would be hid in the covert of God's tent from all pursuit, or be set upon a rock at an elevation inaccessible to his foes. True, he had no longer the asylum of the old home in Bethlehem; in that sense his father and mother had forsaken him (verse 10). But God would gather him, and be father and mother both.

The further references to his extreme need and anguish, to the necessity of being led in a plain path, to the false witnesses who had arisen against him, and who breathed out cruelty—an allusion that may be very well accounted for by Abiathar's account of Doeg's treachery—combine to associate this lovely and pathetic psalm with David's residence in the cave. It is just such a cry as must frequently have broken from his heart in those sad and dark days. Often must the splintered rocks around have heard his strong cryings and tears, and witnessed the awful swoon of his soul, nigh unto death, as he looked down on the abyss from which he was hardly delivered. He could not forget that, by his recent lapse at Gath, he had given cause to God to hide his face from him, to leave him and put him away in anger; but he pleads that, through all those bitter passages of his life, he " believed to see the goodness of the Lord in the land of the living"; and he comforts himself by the reflection that he who sustained his soul with the blessed hope could not fail to realize the vision with which he had allured the wanderer back to himself.

The main objection that obtains against the supposition

that the psalm dates from this period of David's life arises from his mention of the Lord's house, tabernacle, and temple. Still this is not conclusive. We met with the germ of the same thought in the Twenty-third Psalm, where the shepherd-minstrel desired to dwell in the house of the Lord forever. It is not likely that, in his young life, he could have desired seclusion for the rest of his days in the narrow limits of Levitical service. This had been a morbid craving, entirely out of keeping with his heroic soul. Surely, then, the desire for an abiding-place in the house of the Lord, which was the wish of his shepherd days, of his cave experiences, and of his exile when fleeing from Absalom, can only be interpreted as referring to an intimacy of divine fellowship, a constant flow of blessed communication which should supply guidance and direction in all the dark and tortuous pathways of his history.

What fresh and vivid meaning invests his words when read under this light! He desired to abide in communion with God, and to have face-to-face converse with him, as the priests within the precincts of the shrine at Nob. He wished to be able at any moment to inquire of the holy oracle. It was his choice to live so near to God that whenever the divine summons was heard, though in whispers too faint for ordinary ears—

" Seek ye my face,"

he might be near enough to hear it, and reply:

" Thy face, Lord, will I seek."

II. HIS HABITUAL PRACTICE.—When the trembling priest had told his story, David addressed to him words which have a sweet application when placed in the lips of Christ. It is thus that our outcast King, driven beyond the camp, receives each fugitive soul that has recourse to

him. "Abide thou with me," he says, "fear not: for he
that seeketh my life seeketh thy life: but with me thou shalt
be in safeguard."

The special reason that made David glad to welcome
Abiathar was that he brought with him, rescued from the
sack of the little town, the sacred ephod, within which
were the sacred Urim and Thummim. The words signify
"light and perfection"; it is by no means certain what they
refer to. The most probable explanation, however, is the
following:

The high priest's inner garment was a white linen tunic;
over this he wore a blue robe, and above this the ephod,
made of white twined linen, inwrought with blue and purple
and scarlet and gold. To this was affixed the breastplate,
in which were twelve precious stones, corresponding to the
twelve tribes of Israel. In this breastplate, perhaps part of
it, or attached to it, were probably either one or two very
beautiful and resplendent diamonds, through which God
manifested his will. If to any question reverently put to
him by the priest the answer was No, the light in these
precious stones dimmed; if, on the contrary, it was Yes,
they flashed with splendor.

It was obviously a great gain to David to have at hand
this priceless method of communication between Jehovah
and himself. Already Gad was with him, as the representative of the prophetic office; now Abiathar and the ephod
represented the most precious prerogative of the priesthood.
By one or other of these, and probably in these earlier days
especially by the latter, he was able at any moment to know
the will of God.

Do tidings come that the Philistines are plundering
Keilah—he dares not pursue till he has asked the Lord.
Do the cowardly townspeople propose to betray their de-
liverer—he dares not leave the little city till he has received

divine directions to go.   In one of the most awful experiences of his life, when his men spoke of stoning him, instead of taking up his cause, he said to Abiathar, the priest,
" I pray thee, bring hither the ephod." Then Abiathar
brought the ephod to him, and David inquired of the Lord.
Long after he had become the acknowledged king of the
land, in his conflicts with the Philistines he was careful to
inquire of the Lord as to the very method of attack (1 Sam.
xxx. 7; 2 Sam. v. 17–25).

Evidently this was the holy practice of his life: to wait
on God, quelling the fever of his soul, and compelling the
crowd of impetuous thoughts to be in abeyance until time
had been given for the clear disclosure of the divine purpose and plan.   Like a child that dares not take one step
alone, like a traveler in a strange country who is utterly
dependent on his guide, so David lifted up his soul for the
supreme direction which God only can give; to whom the
future is as clearly defined as the past, and from whom
no secrets can be hid.

III. The Lesson for Ourselves.—When Israel came
up out of Egypt they were led across the desert by the
pillar of cloud and fire.   After they were settled in their
own land the Urim and Thummim took its place.   After
a while this method of ascertaining God's will fell into disuse, and the prophets spake as they were moved by the
Holy Ghost.   These, even in the early church, played a
very important part in the ordering of God's people in his
way.

But the voices of the prophets were silenced as the
apostolic age came to a close.   What is our oracle of appeal?   Are pious souls without the means of inquiring of
the Lord, and receiving his clear direction on the difficult
questions perpetually demanding solution?   Not so; for in

one of the last messages given by the ascended Lord to his church, through the Apostle John, it was foretold that he who overcame should receive a *white stone*, and the word *white* means resplendent or lustrous. It may, therefore, denote a diamond, and probably refers to those ancient stones in the high priest's breastplate, that dimmed or flashed with the divine oracles. On them the holy name Jehovah was inscribed in mystic characters; and similarly it is said that on the white stone, which each believer should receive who had overcome in the spiritual conflict against sin and the world, a new name should be written, unknown save to him that received it (Rev. ii. 17).

In other words, each child of God has his own Urim and Thummim stone, which is a conscience void of offense, a heart cleansed in the blood of Christ, a spiritual nature which is pervaded and filled by the Holy Spirit of God.

When we are in doubt or difficulty, when many voices urge this course or the other, when prudence utters one advice and faith another, then let us be still, hushing each intruder, calming ourselves in the sacred hush of God's presence; let us study his Word in the attitude of devout attention; let us lift up our nature into the pure light of his face, eager only to know what God the Lord shall determine—and ere long a very distinct impression will be made, the unmistakable forthtelling of his secret counsel. It is not wise, in the earlier stages of Christian life, to depend on this alone, but to wait for the corroboration of circumstances. But those who have had many dealings with God know well the value of secret fellowship with him, to ascertain his will. The journals of George Fox are full of references to this secret of the Lord, which is with them that fear him, to whom he shows his covenant.

Are you in difficulty about your way? Go to God with your question; get direction from the light of his smile or

the cloud of his refusal. If only you will get alone, where
the lights and shadows of earth cannot interfere, where the
disturbance of self-will does not intrude, where human
opinions fail to reach—and if you will dare to wait there
silent and expectant, though all around you insist on immediate decision or action—the will of God will be made
clear; and you will have a new name in addition, a new
conception of God, a deeper insight into his nature and
heart of love, which shall be for yourself alone—a rapturous
experience, to abide your precious perquisite forever, the
rich guerdon of those long waiting hours.

XIII

Songs Born of Sorrow

(I SAMUEL xxiii.)

"A song of the heart that is broken,
    A song of the sighs and the tears,
The sickness, the want, and the sadness
    Of the days of our pilgrimage years.

"Sweet sings the great choir of sorrow
    The song of the gladness untold,
To Him on the throne of his glory,
    Who wept in the days of old."

H. SEARS.

THE church owes many of her sweetest hymns to the profound anguish which wrung the hearts of her noblest children. The rough feet of trial and pain have stamped, as in the oil-press, hearts whose life-blood is preserved in matchless lyrics. There is no such raw material for songs that live from heart to heart as that furnished by sorrow.

It has been said by a modern writer that, to his thought, the mysterious beauty of music is more wonderful than the prodigality of form and color which overspreads the whole of nature; and he goes on to show that man only develops and liberates the music which is latent in almost all substances, waiting for his coming to give it expression. "Man only develops what was within them, just as the coal which is extracted from the bowels of the earth, when set on fire, merely liberates the heat and light which in the forest it received from the sun." Is not this speechless music—locked within nature, pleading to be let out in song or sound through the agency of man—part of the earnest expectation of the creature which waits for the manifestation of the sons of God?

It is remarkable how many of David's psalms date from those dark and sad days when he was hunted as a partridge upon the mountains. His path may be tracked through the Psalter, as well as in the sacred narrative of his wanderings. Keilah, Ziph, Maon, Engedi, yielded themes for strains which will live forever. To this gifted singer the power was intrusted of eliciting the music that lay concealed in the least congenial haunts. Is it not strange that these wild desolations are now immortal, and that each has contributed chords to the complete music of the soul? We will for a little trace the parallel lines of David's history and song.

I. A CLUSTER OF PSALMS.—*Keilah.*—While sheltering in the forest of Hareth, tidings came of a foray of the Philistines on one of the hapless border towns: "Behold, the Philistines are fighting against Keilah, and they rob the threshing-floors." The year's harvest was at that time spread out for threshing; it was an opportune moment, therefore, for the plunderer. The labors of the year were being carried off, and the cattle "lifted by Israel's bitter and relentless foe." Wrapped in these tidings there was probably a covert appeal for help from one who had often proved himself a wall of defense on the southern frontier. Saul was too far away, and perhaps too intent on his fancied personal wrongs, to be available for the rapid action that was required. David was alert, energetic, near at hand. The appeal to him was not in vain, especially as it was ratified by the divine voice. He arose and went down from the hill-country of Judah into the plains, met the marauders on their return journey, heavily laden with booty and impeded with cattle, smote them with great slaughter, and brought back all the spoil to the rejoicing townsfolk, who, in return for his services, gladly lodged and entertained him and his men.

It was a brief spell of sunshine in a dark and cloudy day, and must have been very welcome to the weary little band. To be again in a town that had "gates and bars" was as welcome an exchange for life in the dens and caves of the earth as the comforts of civilization are after the privations of the Tartar steppes. And this gleam of comfort probably elicited from the minstrel-chieftain the Thirty-first Psalm: "Blessed be the Lord: for he hath showed me his marvelous loving-kindness in a strong city."

Ziph.—His stay in Keilah was brought to a summary close by the tidings—given, perhaps, by Jonathan—that Saul was preparing an expedition to take him, like a trapped bird, even though the city that sheltered his rival were destroyed in the attempt. These tidings were confirmed through the ephod, by which David appealed to the God of Israel; and the further information was communicated that the cowardly and ungrateful townsfolk, when forced to choose between the king and himself, would not scruple to save themselves by surrendering their deliverer. Then David and his men, in number about six hundred, arose and departed out of Keilah, and went whithersoever they could go. Perhaps they broke up into small parties, while the leader, with the more intrepid and devoted of his followers, made his way to the neighborhood of Ziph, about three miles south of Hebron.

This was about the lowest ebb in David's fortunes. The

king was searching for him every day with a malignity
which made it evident that he had come out to seek his
life. Beneath the expressions and formulas of devout
religion which he carefully maintained (xxiii. 7, 21), Saul
secretly cherished the resolve of thwarting the divine purpose. He knew—so Jonathan told his friend in a hurried
interview the two noble youths arranged in the wood of
Ziph—that David would be king over Israel. But this did
not abate his determination to take his life if he could.
What a desperate condition his soul had reached, as the
result of turning itself to its own wild and evil way! And
manifestly David had every reason to fear the outbursts of
the hatred which, in proud defiance, had even set itself
against the will of God.

In addition to this relentless hate there was the meditated
treachery of the Ziphites, who sought to curry favor with
the king by betraying David's lurking-place. Tidings of
their intended falseness came to David, and he moved
farther south to the wilderness of Maon, where a conical
hill gives a far-extended view of the surrounding country.
But to the spot the men of Ziph conducted the king with
such deadly accuracy that, before they could escape, the
little beleaguered band found the hill on which they gathered surrounded by the royal troops, and their escape
rendered impossible. Well for them that a breathless
messenger at this juncture burst in on Saul with the words,
"Haste thee, and come; for the Philistines have made a
raid on the land."

Then David drew a long sigh of relief, and sang the
Fifty-fourth Psalm: "Save me, O God, by thy name, and
judge me by thy might."

Engedi.—From Maon, when the heat of the pursuit was
over, David removed his quarters eastward to the strong-
holds of the wild goat on the shores of the Dead Sea. On

the western shore, midway between north and south, there is a little piece of level ground covered with the rich luxuriance of tropical vegetation. It is jealously fenced in by giant cliffs jutting out into the dark waters of the lake; but its beauty is maintained by a tepid stream which issues from the limestone rock four hundred feet above the glen. It is said that gray weather-beaten stones mark the site of an ancient city, and traces of palms have been discovered incrusted in the limestone. But the tangle of a tropical jungle now reigns supreme. This was David's next resort—Engedi, the haunt of the wild goat—where deep caverns in the steep cliffs, and the abundance of water-supply, furnished two of the most important items in his sparse and frugal program. Here, again, the psalmist sets his experiences to music in two priceless songs—the Fifty-seventh Psalm: "Be merciful unto me, O God: for my soul taketh refuge in thee;" and the One Hundred and Forty-second Psalm: "I cry with my voice unto the Lord; with my voice unto the Lord do I make supplication."

Wilderness experiences also gave rise to other psalms, all of them marked by a recurrence of the same metaphors borrowed from the wilderness and rocky scenery; of the same protestations of innocence; of the same appeals for the overshadowing wing of the Most High; of the same delicately worded references to Saul. Among these are Psalms xi., xiii., xvii., xxii., xxv., lxiv.

II. SOME CHARACTERISTICS OF THESE PSALMS.—We cannot deal with them in detail; but one or two features arrest the most superficial glance.

Their Imagery.—Men are as lions. "My soul is among lions: I lie among them that are set on fire." His soul takes refuge in God, hiding in the shadow of his wings, as he had often seen the eaglets do beneath the broad pinion

of the parent bird. God is his rock; he hides in him, as
his fugitive band in the strong deep sides of the cave. His
divine helper will not let his enemies triumph over him; it
shall happen to them as so often happened to hunters in
those very wilds, when they fell down the crumbling sides
of pits dug to trap the creatures of the forest. At night he
shelters in God; with his psaltery he awakes the dawn.
All these psalms are bathed in imagery and metaphors like
these.

Their Delicate References to Saul.—He does not spare
his epithets for those who goad the king to murderous hate.
The men that watched for his stumbling, that cried, "Report it! report it!" that misrepresented and maligned him,
are dealt with in no hesitating or mincing tones. But of
Saul he says nothing, unless there is a veiled allusion to
him in the plural with which he describes the violent men
that sought after his life. There is a plaintive allusion to
happy days, past forever, when he manifested his profound
sympathy for the king's terrible malady, wearing sackcloth
on his flesh, and humbling his soul with fasting (xxxv. 13);
but there are no words of reproach, no upbraidings, no re-
payment of hate with hate. In this there is an anticipation
of the teaching and temper of Jesus.

There is a conscious rectitude. His conscience was void
of offense toward God and man. If challenged as to
his absolute sinlessness, he would have been the first to
deprecate anything of the sort; instantly he would have
acknowledged that in his rough soldier life he was constantly in need of the propitiating sacrifices, which should
plead for him with God. But, in respect to Saul, or to any
treachery against him or his house, or to any crime deserv-
ing such treatment as that with which he was threatened,
he protested his absolute innocence, and turned confidently
to God, with clean hands and a pure heart, as one who had

not lifted up his soul unto vanity, nor sworn deceitfully (Ps. vii. 3, 4, 5; xxiv.).

There is great evidence of suffering. Of all sources of pain, there is none so hard to bear, that stings so sharply and strikes its poison-fangs so deeply, as the malevolence of our fellows. This is what David suffered from most of all. To his highly sensitive spirit it was the most acute form of torture that, though he was absolutely innocent, though he was willing to give himself to prayer and ministry on their behalf, yet his calumniators pursued him with such unrelenting malice—"Their teeth are spears and arrows, and their tongue a sharp sword."

But his appeal was to God:

> " Save me by thy name;
>   Judge me by thy might."

> " Behold, God is my helper."

> " I will cry unto God most high;
>   Unto God that performeth all things for me.
>   He shall send from heaven, and save me.
>   God shall send forth his mercy and truth."

> " Refuge hath failed me; no man careth for my soul.
>   I cried unto thee, O Lord:
>   I said, Thou art my refuge."

What depths of pathos lie in these stanzas of petition! He does not seek to retaliate or avenge his wrong, but commits himself to Him who judgeth righteously, assured that the Righteous One will shelter him during the time of trial, and ultimately bring out his righteousness as the light, and his judgment as the noonday.

If any should read these lines who are unjustly maligned and persecuted, let them rest in the Lord and wait patiently for him. Some little time may elapse before the hour of deliverance will strike, during which they must wear white robes of stainless innocence and purity (Rev. vi. 11); but presently God will arise and lift the poor out of the dust, the needy from the dunghill, "to make them sit with princes, and inherit the throne of glory." For the needy shall not always be forgotten, nor the expectation of the poor perish forever.

XIV

David's Self-Restraint

(I SAMUEL xxiv., xxvi. ; PSALM xlii. I.)

"Wait! for the day is breaking,
  Though the dull night be long;
Wait! God is not forsaking
  Thy heart. Be strong—be strong!

"Wait! 'tis the key to pleasure
  And to the place of God;
Oh, tarry thou his leisure—
  Thy soul shall bear no load."

C. TOWNSEND.

AS David reviewed his life and recorded his experiences
he was well aware of the innumerable evils that had
encompassed him, of the horrible pit and miry clay out of
which he had been brought up, and of the many who had
sought in vain to destroy his soul; but from all he had been
delivered. He dared not attribute his deliverance to the
quickness of his ingenuity or the agility of his movements;
but to God, and God only. Mark his record of God's
dealings with him, as he stands on the eminence of the
years and looks down and back:

"*He* inclined unto me, and heard my cry.
  He brought me up also out of an horrible pit, out of the miry clay;
  He set my feet upon a rock, and established my goings.
  He hath put a new song in my mouth, even praise unto our God."

And if we further inquire what his attitude was during all these long and sad experiences, he answers:

" I waited patiently for the Lord."

In a recent chapter we saw how David waited *on* the Lord; but there is a clear distinction between this and waiting *for* the Lord, though in practice they are generally conjoined. We wait *on* the Lord by prayer and supplication, looking for the indication of his will; we wait *for* the Lord by patience and submission, looking for the interposition of his hand. It is very needful to learn this lesson of silence, patience, resignation; and it is interesting to remark in the two incidents before us how perfectly David had acquired it, and had learned to wait for the Lord.

I. THE BASIS OF WAITING FOR GOD.—There must be a promise to justify us, or some definite committal of God, on which we can rest as the unmistakable revelation of his purpose. In their last interview, in the wood of Ziph, Jonathan had given this to his friend. He had spoken like a messenger from God. How those words rang in the weary heart that had drunk them in as the parched land drinks water! "Fear not," he had said: "for the hand of Saul my father shall not find thee; and thou shalt be king over Israel, and I shall be next unto thee." He had even said that this, too, was Saul's conviction: "That also Saul my father knoweth."

Besides this, he was conscious of faculty and God-given power; of ability to grasp the helm of the distracted kingdom and guide the sorely tossed bark into calmer waters. As all these corroborations of the original promise came into his heart, he became convinced that God had a great purpose in his life, and settled it in his own mind that he would wait patiently for the Lord to do as he had said, and that he would not lift his finger to secure the kingdom for himself. Jehovah had promised; then he would perform. Whenever the moment came for him to sit on the throne as the acknowledged king of his people, it should be from first to last the divine gift and the divine performance. There should be nothing to hinder God from saying:

> " I have set my king
> Upon my holy hill of Sion."

II. Two Notable Incidents.—*Engedi.*—One afternoon, when Saul, with three thousand men, was in hot pursuit of David, amid the wild and tangled rocks of Engedi, a strange incident put him completely in David's power. It was a time of breathless heat; the sunbeams were striking like swords into the deep wadies and ravines, and every living thing, except, perhaps, the little lizards, had crept away into shelter. For the same reason, or because they desired to elude pursuit, David and his men were in the inmost recesses of an immense cavern. Into that very cave Saul came. His men had gone forward. The intense solitude and silence within and without threw him off his guard; he lingered a little in the entrance.

These caves, says Dr. Thomson, are dark as midnight, and the keenest eyes cannot see five paces inward; but one who has been long within, and is looking toward the entrance, can observe with perfect distinctness all that takes place in that direction. The blinding glare of the sunshine on the limestone cliffs made Saul more than ever unable to detect the forms that lined the cave, while they could perfectly well watch his every movement. How little did the king realize the intense interest with which he was being watched by six hundred pairs of eyes, and the peril to which he was exposed! The whole band was thrilled with excitement.

Now was the opportunity for David to end their wanderings and hardships by one thrust of the spear.   They
whispered, "Seize your opportunity!   Could it have fallen
out more fortunately?   Here is the man who has repeatedly
tried to take your life, and is here with that avowed intent.
Surely the law of God itself exonerates us in taking the life
of those who would take ours!   God himself has undoubtedly brought him here that you should avenge your wrongs
and save further ones."

With great difficulty—and to have been able to do such
a thing showed the immense power he exerted over these
wild strong men—David restrained them and curbed his
own passion, that tore like fire through every vein, and
contented himself with creeping near and cutting off the
skirt of the king's robe, to prove to him afterward how
completely he had been in his power.   But even then, after
Saul had gone forth, and David's men crowded round, full
of sullen remonstrance at his weakness, he was struck with
remorse, and he said to them, "The Lord forbid that I
should do this thing unto my lord, the Lord's anointed, to
put forth mine hand against him, seeing he is the Lord's
anointed."

Hachilah.—Previously at this spot David had been nearly
trapped.   This time the tables were turned.   Once more
Saul, probably instigated by a malign influence, that we
shall consider in our next chapter, was in pursuit of his
rival, "having three thousand chosen men of Israel with
him."   Having ascertained by means of scouts the exact
situation of the royal camp, David went to inspect it in
person from an overhanging cliff.   On the outskirts the
wagons made a rude barricade, within these were the soldiers' quarters, and in the innermost circle Saul and Abner
were posted; but the watches were badly kept, and no
precaution was taken against a sudden attack.

A sudden inspiration seized David, and he proposed to Abishai and Ahimelech the Hittite that they should visit the camp by night. Abishai gladly volunteered to accompany him, and, guided by the clear moonlight, they crept down the hill, crossed the ravine, picked their way through the wagons and the sleeping ranks of the soldiers, stood for a moment whispering over the prostrate form of the king, bore off his spear and water-bottle from Saul's head, and then "gat them away, and no man saw it, nor knew it, neither did any awake; because a deep sleep from the Lord was fallen upon them."

Thus again Saul had been in his power; but he had restrained himself. Abishai could not read him nor understand his secret. To him it seemed a most natural and lawful act for David to take the life of the man who was so infatuated for his destruction. Nay, if David were at all squeamish about killing him with his own hand, surely he could have no objection against Abishai doing it, since he was not personally concerned in the feud. In that whispered colloquy over the sleeping monarch, Abishai had suggested that God had delivered his enemy into his chieftain's hand, and had offered to smite him with his own spear with a stroke so deadly, so instant in its effect, that there would be neither sigh nor groan to awake Abner or his body-guard. But David would not have it.

"No," he said, "I will be no party to this deed. None can smite the Lord's anointed and be guiltless. When his appointed death-hour comes, God will take him, either by some natural process in the palace, or amid the going down of the battle. But my hand shall not curtail his days; I will wait God's time."

On each of these occasions David acted with the magnanimity that became a hero and a saint. He would take no mean advantage of his adversary. He would not retaliate or avenge his wrong. He refused to admit the specious argument that opportunity meant permission, and that license meant liberty. He quieted the impetuous fever of his soul, resisted the subtle temptation of the adversary, and elected to await the slow unfolding of the divine purpose.

III. The Behavior that Waiting for God Induces. —*It restrains from crime.* Bitter indeed had David's remorse been, if he had listened to his comrades and put forth his hand against Saul's life. It would have robbed his harp of all its music. There would then have been some justification for Shimei's cursing words on that dark after-day in his life; but as it was, though they cut him to the quick, they met with no answering response from his conscience. As he searched his heart in the sight of God, he knew that Absalom's rebellion and seizure of his throne could not be, as Shimei suggested, a requital in kind for his dealings with Saul. True, months were still to pass, full of anxiety and suspense, before the coronation shouts rang through the streets of Hebron; but they were forgotten as snow dissolves in the river; and then there was nothing to regret, no gnawing conscience, no death's-head at the bottom of his cup of joy. Be still, O heart! wait for God; this will keep thee from acts and words which, if allowed, would shadow thy whole after-life.

It inspires courage. What an intrepid spirit this was that dared to cry after the king and hold up the skirt of his robe; that challenged the two bravest men of his little army to a feat from which one of them shrank! Ah, the man who is living in the divine purpose has the secret of quenchless courage. He knows that no weapon formed against him shall prosper, and that every tongue that shall rise against him in judgment shall be condemned. He fears nothing, except to do wrong and to grieve God. If in following the prepared path he suddenly comes on the brink of a precipice down which he must cast himself, he does not hesitate to do so, knowing that the angels will swoop beneath and bear him up, so that he shall not dash his foot against a stone.

It gives great rest. Surely it was out of such experiences as these that David wrote the Thirty-seventh Psalm, which, though it belongs to a, later period, forever embalms the conclusions of this. The mellow wisdom of old age gathers up the maxims that were wrought out in the fires of early manhood.

> " Fret not thyself because of evil-doers,
> Neither be thou envious against them that work unrighteousness.
> For they shall soon be cut down like the grass,
> And wither as the green herb."

The exhortations of this exquisite psalm, to trust in the Lord, to delight in the Lord, to roll the way of life on the Lord, to rest in the Lord and wait patiently for him, and especially the repeated injunction not to fret, are all bathed in new meaning when read in the light of these memorable incidents in David's life.

Live on the divine purpose. Be not eager for thyself, but only that God's work should be done. It is certain that he will take care of thy interests, if thou carest for his. Calm thyself as a weaned child; rest thee; sit thee still and trust—God is working out the plan of thy life; thou canst not hurry him; it will only expend the energy of thy soul to no purpose if thou allowest its fever to consume thee; in his own time, the best time, he shall give thee the desires of thine heart.

It induces penitence in others. When David gave such unmistakable evidences of his self-restraint, continued loyalty, and surviving affection, in spite of all that had been done to quench it; when he so clearly established his innocence, and showed the baselessness of the charges made against him; when he appealed with such reverence and sincerity from the calumnies and misrepresentations of earth to the decisions of the divine Judge, the miserable monarch lifted up his voice and wept, and confessed that he had "played the fool, and erred exceedingly." Saul recognized David's nobility; the old chivalrous nature which had so captivated the nation in earlier days flashed out with an expiring flicker; and he went so far as to admit that he would be king. Nothing but such forbearance on David's part could have brought him so near repentance.

It is thus that we may win men still. We win most when we appear to have yielded most, and gain advantages by refusing to take them wrongfully. The man who can wait for God is a man of power, and others will acknowledge it and bend beneath his scepter. To be under authority to God's lofty principle is to have soldiers under us who go and come at our will, and do our bidding.

XV

Cush, a Benjamite

(1 SAMUEL xxvi. 1; PSALM vii.)

> " Who to that bliss aspire
> Must win their way through blood and fire!—
> The writhings of a wounded heart
> Are fiercer than a foeman's dart.
> Oft in life's stillest shade reclining,
> In desolation unrepining,
> Without a hope on earth to find
> A mirror in an answering mind,
> Meek souls these are who little deem
> Their daily strife an angel's theme!"
>
> KEBLE.

IT is somewhat surprising to find Saul in search of David, after the first of the incidents described in the previous chapter. At Engedi there seemed so absolute and entire a reconciliation between them. Saul confessed that David was more righteous than himself; acknowledged that he had dealt well with him; asked that God would reward him; and assured him that he would undoubtedly be king. He even went so far as to make him swear that, when he had come to the throne, he would not destroy his name out of his father's house (xxiv. 21). And yet, after so short a space, he is again on the war-path.

These capricious changes may, of course, have been due to the malady from which he was suffering; but another and more satisfactory explanation has been suggested, and one which casts fresh light on the Seventh Psalm. Dr. Maclaren, whose work on the Psalter has brought the whole church into his debt, is specially emphatic in connecting the psalm with this part of David's history, and indicates its value in helping us to understand the rapid vacillations in Saul's behavior.

It is headed " Shiggaion of David, which he sang unto the Lord." That is, it is an irregular ode; like a stream broken over a bed of rocks and stones, expressing by its uneven measure and sudden changes the emotion of its author. We have often to sing these Shiggaion meters; our songs are frequently broken with sighs and groans; but we do well still to sing with such tunefulness as we may. Happy are they who can find themes for singing to the Lord in every sad and bitter experience!

The title proceeds, " Concerning the words of Cush, a Benjamite." Who was this Cush ? The word means *black*. It may possibly refer to the color of the skin and hair, and been given as a familiar designation to some swarthy Benjamite. Some have supposed that it was David's title for Saul; but the terms of respect in which he ever spoke of the Lord's anointed make that supposition unlikely. Others have referred it to Shimei the Benjamite, whose furious abuse of the king in the hour of his calamity elicited such plaintive resignation from him, such passionate resentment from Abishai; but the style and phraseology belong so evidently to this period of David's life that this supposition also seems untenable.

If the psalm be carefully examined it will be found to bear a close resemblance to the words spoken by David when Saul and he held the brief colloquy outside the cave at Engedi, and afterward at the hill Hachilah.

Indeed, the correspondences are so many and minute

that they establish almost beyond question the date of the psalm as synchronous with the incidents described in the last chapter; and if so, we can infer the cause of Saul's renewed passion. On comparison of psalm and narrative it seems more than likely that Cush was one of Saul's intimate friends and constant companions, and that he was incessantly at work poisoning the king's mind with malignant and deliberate falsehoods about David. When Saul was away from this man, and under the spell of David's noble and generous nature, he laid aside his vindictiveness and responded to the appeals of olden friendship and chivalry; but when he returned to his palace, and Cush had fresh opportunities of influencing him, he yielded to the worst side of his character, and resumed his desperate attempt to thwart the divine purpose. Thus like a shuttlecock he was tossed to and fro between the two men; now inclined to mercy by David, and then to vengeance by Cush.

It is quite likely that many of those who shall read these lines will be able to understand, by bitter experiences, the anguish of David's soul from this cause. You too have a Cush in the circle of your life who is constantly circulating baseless and calumnious statements concerning you; poisoning the minds of those who otherwise would be well disposed, and suggesting questions, suspicious misunderstandings of your purest and most untainted actions. Such slanderers are to be found in the salons of modern society, as in the palace of the first king of Israel, and cause as much exquisite torture to sensitive and tender natures to-day as to David in the wilds of Engedi. Let us learn how to deal with such.

I. SEARCH YOUR HEART TO SEE IF THESE SLANDERS HAVE FOUNDATION IN FACT.—It may be that there is more truth in these hurtful words than you are inclined, at

first sight, to admit.   Would it not be wise to ask if it be
so, before dismissing them, or treating them with disdain ?
Perhaps those quick, envious eyes have discerned weak-
nesses in your character, of which your closest friends are
aware, but they have shrunk from telling you; for love is
quick to notice the weak points in the beloved, though it
is not always true to indicate and rebuke.   The supreme
love alone girds itself to the task of washing the feet of its
friends.   It is a good rule, before you destroy the anony-
mous letter, or dismiss the unkind statement which has been
going the round of your society, to sit down before the
judgment-seat of Christ, and in its white light ask yourself
whether you can say with David:

> " My shield is with God,
> Who saveth the upright in heart."

II. IF THERE IS NO BASIS FOR THEM, REJOICE! — Always remember, when men revile you, and persecute you,
and say all manner of evil against you falsely—first, that
you are in the succession of the prophets and saints of
every age, and may be assured that you are on the right
track ; and secondly, that out of this, according to the express words of Christ, you may extract that blessedness
which is richer and deeper than the world's joy, that passes
like a summer brook.

How thankful we should be that God has kept us from
being actually guilty of the things whereof we are accused!
We might have done them, and worse.   It was only by his
grace that we have been withheld.   That we have the witness of good conscience, and of his Spirit in our hearts,
should be a perennial source of gladness.

III. TAKE SHELTER IN THE RIGHTEOUS JUDGMENT OF
GOD.—We are his servants, and if he is satisfied with us,

why should we break our hearts over what our fellow-servants say? He put us into the positions we occupy, and if he please to keep us there, all that men may say or do will be unavailing to dislodge us. It is, after all, but a small matter with us to be judged of man's judgment; yea, we judge not our own selves, but he that judgeth us is the Lord. He only can properly determine the quality of our lives, because to him alone are the hidden things known which give the real clue to rightness or wrongness.

IV. ABJURE MORE COMPLETELY THE CARNAL LIFE.—Why do we smart under these unkind and slanderous words, which are as baseless as uncharitable? Is it not because we set too high a value upon the favor and applause of men? Is there not a deadly fear of being despised and condemned? Does not the world still live within us, revealing the tenacity of its hold in this mortification and shame? Is this being crucified to the world and the world crucified to us?

If we were really nothing, and God were all in all; if the Spirit and the Lamb of God were dominant in our inner life; if we were dead to the flesh, with its affections and lusts, and alive only to God, surely it would be a matter of indifference what became of our good name in the lips of foolish and sinful men. Here, then, there is a revelation of a deeper death to be realized; let us not flinch from it, but be willing to fall into the ground and die to our reputation, as Jesus did, who endured the contradiction of sinners against himself, and of whom they spoke as in league with Beelzebub, the prince of demons.

We must choose death in all those forms in which our Master knew it; that, having been planted in the likeness of his death, we may be also in the likeness of his resurrection.

V. Leave God to Vindicate your Good Name. —
Any unjust imputation or stigma that rests on us is part of
the evil of the world, and a manifestation of its inveterate
badness; it is a grief and care to God; it is part of the
burden which he is carrying ever; it is impossible for us to
cope with or remove it; it is useless to retaliate or revenge.
Like Jesus, we may meekly ask the false accuser to establish
his untrue charges, or we may meet them with our steadfast
denial; but when we have done this, and we shall find it of
little avail, there is no more to do but wait patiently till God
arise to avenge our wrong and vindicate our characters.

It was so that David acted, even in those twilight days.
He appealed to the righteous God who trieth the hearts and
reins; believed that he would gird on his armor, whetting
his sword and bending his bow against those who repented
not of their hatred against his saints.   The psalmist had a
clear apprehension of the immutable law that the wicked-
ness of the wicked would come to an end; that his mischief
would return on his own head; that the trapper of the
saints would fall into his own snare; while they would be
established, and their character cleared.   It was so that
Jesus bore himself: "When he was reviled, he reviled not
again; when he suffered, he threatened not; but committed
himself to him that judgeth righteously."

Such is the true and wisest policy.   Be still; give place
unto wrath; concern thyself rather with the misery of that
soul from which these wild words proceed; think more of
this than of thy wrongs; let thy heart be exercised with a
great tenderness toward him; if he hunger, feed him; if he
thirst, give him drink; try to overcome the evil of his heart
by thy generous good; and leave vindication and vengeance alike to God, whose prerogative is to plead the cause
of the innocent and defenseless, while he will repay the
wrong-doer in due time.

XVI

𝔄 𝔠𝔬𝔬𝔩 𝔥𝔞𝔫𝔡 𝔬𝔫 𝔞 𝔥𝔬𝔱 𝔥𝔢𝔞𝔡

(1 SAMUEL xxv.)

" Calm me, my God, and keep me calm;
    Let thine outstretchèd wing
Be like the shade of Elim's palm,
    Beside her desert spring.

" Calm in the sufferance of wrong,
    Like Him who bore my shame;
Calm 'mid the threatening, taunting throng,
    Who hate thy holy name."

H. BONAR.

THE tidings passed throughout the land, like fire in
    prairie-grass, that Samuel was dead; and Israel, recog-
nizing its unity in the common loss, gathered to lament the
prophet and saint, and perform the last honoring rites. To
his worth and service was accorded the unusual tribute of
interment within the precincts of his own house at Ramah,
on the heights of Benjamin. In all likelihood an amnesty
was proclaimed, and David came to take part in the obse-
quies of his master and friend. He did not, however, dare
to trust himself in such near proximity to Saul a moment
longer than was absolutely essential; and as soon as all
was over, he started again for the sparsely populated region
of Paran, at the extreme south of Judah. To those border-
lands, so long desolated by border warfare through the
incursions of the Philistines and Amalekites, his advent

brought tranquillity and safety. The sheep-masters had every reason to be grateful for his protection; and, as one well put it, "The men were very good unto us, and we were not hurt, neither missed we anything, as long as we were conversant with them. They were a wall unto us both by night and day, all the while we were with them keeping the sheep."

Where such services were accepted and counted upon, it was obviously fair, and, indeed, according to the custom of the time, that some recompense in kind should be made. It was a tacit understanding, an unwritten law; and David was perfectly justified in sending ten young men to greet the opulent sheep-master Nabal in the day of prosperity, to which the exertions of himself and his men had so largely contributed, to remind him of his obligations, and ask whatsoever might come readily to his hand to give. Nabal's churlish treatment of this request touched David to the quick, and led up to an incident which, as recorded by the sacred historian, is one of the most charming idyls of Scripture, fragrant as the flowers of Alpine pastures, and fresh as a summer morn.

The story centers in Nabal, David, and Abigail.

I. NABAL, THE CHURL.—His character is drawn, after the manner of Scripture, in three or four bold outline-strokes, and need not detain us. In every society men of this type are to be encountered, overbearing to their inferiors, intolerable in prosperity, drunken in carouse, abject in misfortune; who fly out with flout and sneer when they think themselves secure, but whose heart cringes before reverse. What an apt thumb-nail sketch is given of the whole race of Nabals in the confidential remark passed between his servant and his wife: "He is such a son of Belial, that one cannot speak to him"!

He was very great, the historian says.   But it was the
meanest kind of greatness, consisting, not in what he was
in character or had achieved in valiant deed, but in the
number of sheep and goats that bore his brand over the
pasture-lands of the south.   There are four kinds of greatness; young men, choose the best for your life-aim!   It is
little to be great in possessing; better to be great in doing;
better still to conceive and promulgate great thoughts; but
best to be great in character   Aim at the greatness of
which Heaven takes account.   It was where self-mastery,
Holy Ghost fullness, and service to mankind met that the
angel said, " He shall be great in the sight of the Lord."

He was a fool, his wife said.   " As his name is, so is he;
Nabal is his name, and folly is with him."   Poor woman!
She had had every reason for speaking thus bitterly of
him; and she was a sweet woman, too, not likely to speak
in these terms of her husband unless his rude, cruel hands
had wantonly broken down the last remnant of wifely respect and love.   He surely must have sat for the full-length
portrait of the fool in our Lord's parable, who thought his
soul could take its ease and be merry because a few big
barns were full.   There are appetites and longings in the
soul which good dinners cannot satisfy; there are cravings
which will not be appeased merely because we can see our
way to three meals a day as long as we live.

He was a man of Belial, his servant said; and, indeed,
his treatment of David's modest request well bore out the
character.   It was rude, uncourteous, uncivil.   He could
not have been ignorant of the causes which had forced
David into his wandering, arduous life; but he ignored
them, and chose to put forward the most cruel and harsh
construction.   He as good as said that David was raising
a revolt against his master Saul; virtuously covered his
refusal beneath a show of loyal devotion to law and gov-

ernment, which was intended to suggest an extremely
unpleasant alternative for David; and finally asserted his
preference to give his bread and flesh to those who, like
his shearers, had worked for them, rather than to a lot of
vain fellows who were hanging idly about to live on the
ripe fruit that might fall into their mouths.

He seems to have had no compunction for his churlish
speeches, no idea of the consequences they might involve.
As soon as the words were spoken they were forgotten; and
in the evening of the day on which they were spoken we
find him in his house, holding a feast like the feast of a
king, his heart merry with wine, and altogether so stupid
that his wife told him nothing, less or more, till the morning
light.

II. DAVID, PRECIPITATE AND PASSIONATE. — One of the
most characteristic features in David's temper and behavior
through all these weary years was his self-control. He
waited patiently for the Lord. Year after year he stayed
himself on God's promise, and left him to fulfil the word
on which he had caused him to hope. When summoned
to relieve Ziklag, or warned to leave it, as well as on other
occasions, he showed the utmost deliberation, calling for
prophet or priest, and seeking to ascertain the divine will
before stirring a step. On two occasions he had controlled
himself when Saul lay in his power, and refused to take his
life. But the rampart of self-restraint built by long habit
went down, like a neglected sea-wall, before the sudden
paroxysm of passion which Nabal's insulting words aroused.
In hot fury he said to his men, " Gird ye on every man his
sword." And they girded on every man his sword, and
David also girded on his sword, and there went up after
David about four hundred men. He doubtless argued
with himself, as they marched rapidly through the silent

wolds: "I am justified in this act; there is no reason why this man should treat me thus; he has returned evil for good, and added reviling and reproach; it is intolerable. I must assert my self-respect, and let this neighborhood see that I am not going to be trifled with. I will bear from the king what I will suffer from no living man else."

At this hour David was on the brink of committing a crime which would have cast a dark shadow on all his after-years. In calmer, quieter, holier hours it would have been a grief to him, and an offense of heart, to have shed blood causelessly, and avenged himself, instead of leaving it to the Lord to sling out the souls of his enemies as from the hollow of a sling. From this shame, sorrow, and disgrace he was saved by that sweet and noble woman, Abigail.

III. ABIGAIL, THE BEAUTIFUL INTERCESSOR.—She was a woman of good understanding and of a beautiful countenance—a fit combination. Her character had written its legend on her face. The two things do not always go together. There are many beautiful women wholly destitute of good understanding; just as birds of rarest plumage are commonly deficient in the power of song. But a good understanding, which is moral rather than intellectual, casts a glow of beauty over the plainest features.

It is remarkable how many Abigails get married to Nabals. God-fearing women, tender and gentle in their sensibilities, high-minded and noble in their ideals, become tied in an indissoluble union with men for whom they can have no true affinity, even if they have not an unconquerable repugnance. In Abigail's case this relationship was in all probability not of her choosing, but the product of the Oriental custom which compelled a girl to take her father's choice in the matter of marriage. As a mere child she may have come into Nabal's home, and become bound to him by an apparently inevitable fate. In other ways which involve equally little personal choice, compelled by the pressure of inexorable circumstances, misled by the deceitful tongue of flattery, her instinctive hesitancy overcome by the urgency of friends, a woman may still find herself in Abigail's pitiful plight. To such a one there is but one advice—you must stay where you are. The dissimilarity in taste and temperament does not constitute a sufficient reason for leaving your husband to drift. You must believe that God has permitted you to enter on this awful heritage, partly because this fiery ordeal was required by your character, and partly that you might act as a counteractive influence. You must stay as you are. It may be that some day your opportunity will come, as it came to Abigail. In the meantime do not allow your purer nature to be bespotted or besmeared. You can always keep the soul clean and pure. Bide your time; and amid the weltering waste of inky water be like a pure fountain rising from the ocean depths.

But if any young girl of good sense and earnest aspirations who reads these lines secretly knows that, if she had the chance, she would wed a carriage and pair, a good position, or broad acres, irrespective of character, let her remember that to enter the marriage bond with a man, deliberately and advisedly, for such a purpose is a profanation of the divine ideal, and can end only in one way. She will not raise him to her level, but sink to his; her marble will not change his clay, but coarsen to it.

Nabal's servants knew the quality of their mistress, and could trust her to act wisely in the emergency which was upon them; so they told her all. She immediately grasped the situation, despatched a small procession of provision-bearers along the way that David must come, and followed

them immediately on her ass. She met the avenging warriors by the covert of the mountain, and the interview was
as creditable to her woman's wit as to her grace of heart.
The lowly obeisance of the beautiful woman at the young
soldier's feet; the frank confession of the wrong that had
been done; the expression of thankfulness that so far he
had been kept from blood-guiltiness and from avenging his
own wrongs; the depreciation of the generous present she
brought as only fit for his servants; the chivalrous appreciation of his desire to fight only the battles of the Lord
and to keep an unblemished name; the sure anticipation
of the time when his fortunes would be secured and his
enemies silenced; the suggestion that in those coming days
he would be glad to have no shadow on the sunlit hills of
his life, no haunting memory—all this was as beautiful and
wise and womanly as it could be, and brought David back
to his better self. Frank and noble as he always was, he
did not hesitate to acknowledge his deep indebtedness to
this lovely woman, and to see in her intercession the
gracious arrest of God. "And David said to Abigail,
Blessed be the Lord, the God of Israel, which sent thee
this day to meet me: and blessed be thy wisdom, and
blessed be thou, which hast kept me this day from blood-
guiltiness, and from avenging myself with my own hand."

What a revelation this is of the ministries with which God
seeks to avert us from our evil ways! They are sometimes
very subtle and slender, very small and still; sometimes a
gentle woman's hand laid on our wrist, the mother remind-
ing us of her maternity, the wife of early vows, the child
with its pitiful, beseeching look; sometimes a thought, holy,
pleading, remonstrating. Ah, many a time we had been
saved actions which have caused lasting regret had we only
heeded. And above all these voices and influences there
has been the gracious arresting influence of the Holy

Spirit, striving with passion and selfishness, calling us to a nobler, better life. Blessed Spirit, come down more often by the covert of the hill, and stay us in our mad career; and let us not press past thee to take our own wild way, and we shall have reason for ceaseless gratitude.

The idyl ended happily. Nabal died in an apoplectic fit, caused by his debauch, or his anger at his wife's treatment of David and his men; and David made proposals of marriage to the woman to whom he owed so much, which she gracefully and humbly accepted, not thinking herself meet for such high honor. "Behold," she said, "thy hand-maid is a servant to wash the feet of the servants of my lord." I suppose that in this life or the next all God's idyls end happily. That, at least, is one cherished article of my creed.

XVII

A Fit of Mistrust

(I SAMUEL xxvii.)

" Ever thus the spirit must,
  Guilty in the sight of Heaven,
  With a keener woe be riven,
For its weak and sinful trust
In the strength of human dust;
And its anguish thrill afresh
  For each vain reliance given
To the failing arm of flesh."
                        WHITTIER.

THE psalms which, with more or less probability, may
   be assigned to this period of David's life are marked
with growing sadness and depression. Among them may
be reckoned the Tenth, Thirteenth, Seventeenth, Twenty-
second, Twenty-fifth, Forty-fourth, and perhaps the Fortieth
and Sixty-ninth. Those of the first group have many features in common. The scenery of the wilderness, the psalmist like a hunted wild thing, the perpetual insistence on his
innocence and invocation of Jehovah's interference, the
bitter description of his sorrows—such are the characteristic
features of these psalms. But, besides, there is a tone of
despair:

   " Why standest thou afar off, O Lord ?
   Why hidest thou thyself in times of trouble ? " (x. 1).

" How long, O Lord ?   Wilt thou forget me forever ?
How long wilt thou hide thy face from me ? " (xiii. 1).

" My God, my God, why hast thou forsaken me ?
Why art thou so far from helping me, and from the words of my
    roaring ? " (xxii. 1).

" Save me, O God ;
For the waters are come in unto my soul.
I sink in deep mire, where there is no standing :
I am come into deep waters, where the floods overflow me " (lxix. 1).

These notes are sad, plaintive, and despairful; it is as
though the sufferer were near the limits of his endurance.
It seemed hopeless to effect any permanent alteration in
Saul's feelings toward him, so long as Cush and Doeg and
Abner, and others who had proved themselves his inveterate foes, were able so readily to instil their poison into the
royal ear.   It had become so increasingly difficult to elude
the hot pursuit of the royal troops, whom long practice had
familiarized with his hiding-places and haunts.   And it became more and more perplexing to find sustenance for the
large body of followers now attached to him.   Every day
he had to provide for six hundred men, besides women and
children; and the presence of these more tender souls made
it perilously difficult to maintain a perpetual condition of
migration or flight.   He had now two wives; and from
what is said of the sack of Ziklag, shortly afterward, we
should judge that the larger proportion of the outlawed
band consisted of those who had wives and sons and
daughters and property (xxx. 3, 6, 19, 22).

In other days of healthier faith these considerations
would not have availed to shake the constancy of his
much-tried soul.   He would have stayed himself upon his
God, and been strengthened with all power unto all
patience and long-suffering with joy.   But of late his faith

had become impaired and the loins of his godly courage slackened, so that he said in his heart, " I shall now perish one day by the hand of Saul: there is nothing better for me than that I should escape into the land of the Philistines; and Saul shall despair of me, to seek me any more in all the borders of Israel: so shall I escape out of his hand."

LET US EXAMINE THIS SUDDEN RESOLUTION.—*It was the suggestion of worldly policy.* " David said in his heart." On other occasions, as we have observed more than once, it had been his wont to summon the priest with the sacred ephod, or to inquire of God through Gad; but in this resolution he had recourse to neither the one nor the other. In the matter of Nabal he had acted under the sudden impulse of passion; here under that of panic. He looked at circumstances, perhaps listened to the counsels of men who were attracted to him by the qualities of daring, bravery, and frank generosity, which made him the popular hero of his time, but had no sympathy with the deeper springs of his life in God and faith and prayer. Never act in a panic, nor allow man to dictate to thee; calm thyself and be still; force thyself into the quiet of thy closet until the pulse beats normally and the scare has ceased to perturb. When thou art most eager to act is the time when thou wilt make the most pitiable mistakes. Do not say in thine heart what thou wilt or wilt not do; but wait upon God until he makes known his way. So long as that way is hidden, it is clear that there is no need of action, and that he accounts himself responsible for all the results of keeping thee where thou art.

It was very dishonoring to God. Had he not sworn to make him king, to cast forth his enemies as out of a sling, and to give him a sure house? Had not these promises been confirmed by Samuel, Jonathan, Abigail, and Saul himself? Had not the golden oil designated him as God's anointed? How impossible it was that God should lie or forget his covenant! By immutable pledges his almighty Friend had bound himself, seeking to give his much-tried child strong consolation, if only he would remain within the sheltering walls of the refuge-harbor which these assurances constituted; and it was easier for heaven and earth to pass away than for one jot or tittle of the divine engagements to become invalid.

Surely, then, it was unworthy of David to say, in effect: "I am beginning to fear that God has undertaken more than he can carry through. True, he has kept me hitherto; but I question if he can make me surmount the growing difficulties of my situation. Saul will, sooner or later, accomplish his designs against me; it is a mistake to attempt the impossible. I have waited till I am tired; it is time to use my own wits and extricate myself while I can from the nets that are being drawn over my path."

The resolution must have given great rejoicing to many of his followers; but all devout souls must have felt that the leader's despairing confession was in sad contrast to his exhortation, so repeatedly insisted upon, to wait on God.

> " None that wait on thee shall be ashamed:
>   They shall be ashamed that transgress without cause."

How much easier it is to indicate a true course to others in hours of comparative security than to stand to it under a squall of wind! Dr. Tauler, the great preacher of Strassburg, before his second and deeper conversion, could be excelled by none in his delineation of the virtues of humility and self-denial; yet when the humble traveler from the Oberland remonstrated with him for loving one creature, himself, more than God, he was offended, and his proud heart arose within him. It is an experience through which

most of us have to pass—the contrast between speech and
possession ; between thinking we have and having ; between
our directions to others and our own behavior when the
dark waters are sweeping over our soul.

It was highly injurious.   Philistia was full of idol temples
and idolatrous priests (2 Sam. v. 21).   It lay outside the inheritance of the Lord, the sacred land of Palestine, deemed
by the pious Israelites of those days to be the special loca-
tion and abiding-place of the Most High, and to be ban-
ished from whose sacred borders seemed like going into a
wild and desolate land of estrangement and God-abandon-
ment.   What fellowship could David look for with the
divine Spirit who had chosen Israel for his people and
Jacob for the lot of his inheritance?   How could he sing
the Lord's songs in a strange land?   What share could he
claim in the sacrifices which sent up the thin spiral of smoke
on the sites of Nob or Kirjath-jearim?   Besides, their perpetual familiarity with the rites and iniquities of idolatry
could not but exert an unwholesome and altogether disastrous effect on the minds of the unstable in his band.
Poison must have been injected into many hearts, that
wrought disastrously in after years.   What was harmless
enough in the case of David, who knew that an idol was
nothing in the world, was perilous in the extreme to the
weak consciences in his train, which were defiled by what
they saw and heard.

*It was the entrance on a course that demanded the perpet-
ual practice of deceit.*   He was received at Gath with open
arms.   Before, when he had sought the shelter of the court
of Achish, he had but a handful of companions ; now he
was the leader of a formidable band of warriors, who might
easily turn the scale of strength in the long struggle between
Israel and Philistia.   "And David dwelt with Achish, he
and his men, every man with his household."

This proximity to the royal palace and the court became, however, extremely irksome to the Hebrews. Their movements were always under inspection, and it was difficult to preserve their autonomy and independence. Finally, therefore, David asked that one of the smaller towns might be assigned to him; and to his great comfort received permission to settle at Ziklag, a town in the south country, originally allotted to Judah, then transferred to Simeon, and latterly captured by the Philistines, but not occupied by them (Josh. xv. 31; xix. 5; 1 Chron. iv. 30).

The sense of security and relief to these hunted men must have been very great as they found themselves within the slender fortifications of the little town. For long they had known no settled home, their life full of alarm and flight, the weapon always at their side or in their hand, the senses alert to the rustle of a leaf or the slightest movement in the covert; from all these there was now a grateful pause. For sixteen months they had a measure of repose and safety. The old men and women sat in the streets, and the shouts of merry children in their play were no longer instantly and jealously hushed lest they should attract the scouts of the royal army. "It was told Saul that David was fled to Gath: and he sought no more again for him."

David's mind was, however, kept on the stretch, constantly at work weaving a tissue of duplicity and cruelty. He had really no love for Achish, no zeal for the maintenance of his rule; he had not deserted the chosen people, though he had fled before Saul; in his deepest soul he was still a Hebrew of the Hebrews. Maintenance for himself and his followers must, of course, be provided; and in those days of wild border war nothing was more obvious, to the Philistines at least, than to raid the land on which he had turned his back. This, of course, he would not do; and so he turned his sword on the petty tribes of the south country, who were in alliance with the Philistines, but the hereditary foes of his own people. Among these were the Geshurites and Gezrites and the Amalekites, all nomad tribes, living by plunder. To obviate any report of his proceedings reaching the ears of Achish, David was compelled to adopt the cruel and sanguinary policy of saving neither man nor woman alive; and when Achish, by virtue of his feudal lordship, required of him an account of his expedition, he said evasively that he had been raiding against the south of Judah, and instanced tribes which were known to be under the direct protection of Israel. The fact of his having brought back no captives, the most valuable part of booty, was reckoned by the Philistines a proof of the passionate hate with which he regarded his countrymen, making him forego the pecuniary advantage accruing from the sale of slaves, rather than the satisfaction of beholding their dying anguish. "And Achish believed David, saying, He hath made his people Israel utterly to abhor him; therefore he shall be my servant forever."

The whole behavior of David at this time was utterly unworthy of his high character as God's anointed servant. *It was also a barren time in his religious experience.* No psalms are credited to this period. The sweet singer was mute. He probably acquired a few new strains of music, or even mastered some fresh instruments, while sojourning at Gath, the memory of which is perpetuated in the term *Gittith*, a term which frequently occurs in the inscriptions of the psalms composed afterward. But who would barter a song for a melody, a psalm for a guitar? It was a poor exchange. There was something in the air of those low-

land plains that closed the utterances of the sweet voice
that had sung to God amid the hills of Judah and the caves
of Ain-jedi.

How precisely do these symptoms of old-time declension
and relapse correspond with those which we have observed
in ourselves and others! The way of faith may be irksome to the flesh, but it is free and glad to the spirit. It
may have to trace its steps with difficulty among the hills,
but a new song is in its mouth, of praise and thanksgiving.
But when we descend to the lowlands of expediency and
worldly policy, a blight comes on the landscape of the soul,
a silence on the song of the heart.

From that moment we are left to maintain our position
by our own scheming and planning; we ask God to help
us, but dare not count on him absolutely to provide for us;
we are driven into tight corners, from which we escape by
subterfuge and duplicity, such as we in our souls despise;
we realize that we have purchased our deliverance from the
pressure of adverse circumstances at too great a cost, and
have bartered the smile of God for that of Achish, so soon
to be turned from us; the munitions of divine protection for
the walls of Ziklag, over the ruins of which we shall soon
be weeping scalding tears.

XVIII

The Mercy of God that Led to Repentance

(1 SAMUEL xxix., xxx.)

" Prostrate your soul in penitential prayer!
  Humble your heart beneath the mighty hand
  Of God, whose gracious guidance oft shall lead
  Through sin and crime the changed and melted heart,
  To sweet repentance and the sense of him."

CLOUGH.

THROUGHOUT that season of declension and relapse which we have been considering the loving mercy of God hovered tenderly over David's life. When we believe not, he remains faithful—he cannot deny himself; and when his servants are wandering far afield, sowing for themselves thistledown, and piercing themselves through with bitter sorrows, he is encompassing their path and their lying down, solicitous of heart and compassionate, exhibiting the tenderest traits of his mercy and pity, as though to win them back to himself.

This is particularly illustrated by the present stage of David's history. There was a special focusing of divine gentleness and goodness to withdraw him from his purpose, to keep back his soul from the pit and his life from perishing with the sword. We will now trace the successive stages in this loving process of divine restoration; and as we do so, we will believe that all these things doth God work still, to bring back our souls from the pit, that we may be enlightened with the light of life. In us also David's words shall be verified, spoken as he reviewed this part of his career from the eminence of prosperity and glory to which God's goodness afterward raised him: "Thy gentleness hath made me great." God's restoring mercy was evident:

I. IN INCLINING STRONG AND NOBLE MEN TO IDENTIFY THEMSELVES WITH DAVID'S CAUSE.—"Now these are they," says the chronicler, "that came to David to Ziklag, while he yet kept himself close because of Saul the son of Kish: and they were among the mighty men, helpers in war" (1 Chron. xii. 1). And he proceeds to enumerate them. Some came from Saul's own tribe, experienced marksmen, who could use, with equal dexterity, the right hand and the left in slinging stones and in shooting arrows from the bow. Some came from the eastern bank of the Jordan, swimming in at the flood, mighty men of valor, men trained for war, whose faces were like the faces of lions, and they were as swift as roes among the mountains. Some came from Benjamin and Judah, assuring David that there was no ground for his suspicions of their loyalty. What a manly, generous ring there was in those reassuring words as uttered by their leader, Amasai, and which were probably the expression of the feelings of all the contingents of heroes which at this time rallied around David's standard: "Thine are we, David, and on thy side, thou son of Jesse: peace, peace be unto thee, and peace to thine helpers; for thy God helpeth thee" !

Evidently the spirit of discontent was abroad in the land. The people, weary of Saul's oppression and misgovernment, were beginning to realize that the true hope of Israel lay in the son of Jesse. They therefore went out to him without the camp, bearing his reproach, content to forfeit everything they possessed in the assurance that they would receive it all again, and a hundredfold besides, when he came by his own. Thus from day to day " there came to David to help him, until it was a great host, like the host of God."

Thus, in silence and secrecy, loyal and true hearts are gathering around our blessed Lord, the center of whose kingdom is not earthly, but heavenly; who has gone away to receive a kingdom, but who shall certainly return; and when he is manifested in his kingly glory, then shall they also be manifested with him. Who, then, are willing to leave the tottering realm of the prince of this world, soon to be shattered on the last great battle-field of time, and identify themselves with the kingdom of the Son of David, which is destined to endure as long as the sun?

II. IN EXTRICATING HIS SERVANT FROM THE FALSE POSITION INTO WHICH HE HAD DRIFTED.—The Philistines suddenly resolved on a forward policy. They were aware of the disintegration which was slowly dividing Saul's kingdom, and had noticed with secret satisfaction the growing numbers of mighty men who were leaving it to seek identification with David, and therefore, presumably, with themselves. Not content, therefore, with the border hostilities that had engaged them so long, they resolved to follow the course of the maritime plain—the long stretch of low-lying land on the shores of the Mediterranean—and to strike a blow in the very heart of the land, the fertile plain of Esdraelon, destined to be one of the greatest battle-fields of the world, drenched with the blood of great leaders, as Sisera, Saul, and Joash, and of vast hosts, Philistine and Hebrew, Egyptian and Assyrian, Roman and Maccabean, Saracen and Anglo-Saxon. " The Philistines gathered their hosts together for warfare to Aphek: and the Israelites pitched by the fountain which is in Jezreel."

When this campaign was being meditated, the guileless king assured David that he should accompany him. This was perhaps said as a mark of special confidence. It would have been foolhardy on the part of Achish to associate David with himself on such an expedition, had he not conceived the most absolute confidence in his integrity. He had seen no fault in his protégé from the first hour of his coming into his court, but had looked on him as an angel of God; he had no hesitation, therefore, in summoning him to march beside him, and even to be captain of his body-guard. "Therefore will I make thee keeper of mine head forever." It was a relief to the gentle nature of the king to turn from his imperious lords to this generous, open-hearted soul, and intrust himself to his strong care.

It was, however, a very critical juncture with David. He had no alternative but to follow his liege lord into the battle; but it must have been with a sinking heart. It looked as though he would be forced to fight Saul, from whom for so many years he had fled; and Jonathan, his beloved friend; and the chosen people, over whom he hoped one day to rule. He could not but reply evasively, and with forced composure and gaiety, "Thou shalt know what thy servant will do;" but every mile of those fifty or sixty which had to be traversed must have been trodden with lowering face and troubled heart. There was no hope for him in man. It may be that already his heart was turning in eager prayer to God, that he would extricate him from the net that his sins had woven for his feet; and in the evasiveness of the reply he gave to Achish there is a trace of glimmering hope that God would yet show a way of escape from his fearful dilemma.

If by your mistakes and sins you have reduced yourself to a false position like this, do not despair; hope still in God. Confess and put away your sin, and humble yourself before him, and he will arise to deliver you. You may have destroyed yourself, but in him will be your help. "If any of thine outcasts [outcasts because of their disobedience and apostasy] be in the uttermost parts of heaven, from thence will the Lord thy God gather thee, and from thence will he fetch thee: and the Lord thy God will bring thee into the land which thy fathers possessed, and thou shalt possess it; and he will do thee good, and multiply thee above thy fathers."

An unexpected door of hope was suddenly opened in this valley of Achor. When Achish reviewed his troops in Aphek, after the lords of the Philistines had passed on by hundreds and by thousands, David and his men passed on in the rearward with the king. This aroused the jealousy and suspicion of the imperious Philistine princes, and they came to Achish with fierce words and threats: "What do these Hebrews here? Make the man return, that he may go back to the place where thou hast appointed him, and let him not go down with us to the battle." In vain Achish pleaded on the behalf of his favorite; the Philistines would have none of it. They pointed out how virulent a foe he had been, and how tempting the opportunity for him to purchase reconciliation with Saul by turning traitor in the fight. In the end, therefore, the king had to yield. It cost him much to inform David of the inevitable decision to which he was driven; but he little realized with what a burst of relief his announcement was received. We can imagine David saying to himself as he left the royal pavilion:

> " My soul is escaped as a bird from the snare of the fowler.
> The snare is broken, and I am escaped."

He made a show of injured innocence: "What have I done? and what hast thou found in thy servant so long as

I have been before thee unto this day, that I may not go
and fight against the enemies of my lord the king?" But
his heart was not with his words; and it was with unfeigned
satisfaction that he received the stringent command to depart from the camp with the morning light. As in the gray
dawn he stealthily mustered his men to start, did he not
fling one glance as far as the mists permitted to the camp
of Israel, where the lion-heart of the beloved Jonathan was
doubtless preparing itself for the fight? Oh, to have been
permitted to be beside him in repelling one of the most
formidable invasions of their lives!

III. BY THE DIVINE DEALINGS WITH HIM IN RESPECT
TO THE BURNING OF ZIKLAG.—It was by God's great mercy
that the Philistine lords were so set against the continuance
of David in their camp. They thought that they were exe-
cuting a piece of ordinary policy, dictated by prudence
and foresight; little realizing that they were the shears by
which God was cutting the meshes of David's net. Their
protest was lodged at exactly the right moment; had it
been postponed by but a few hours, David had been involved in the battle, or had not been back in time to over-
take the Amalekites red-handed in the sack of Ziklag.

As David was leaving the battle-field a number of the
men of Manasseh, who appear to have deserted to Achish,
were assigned to him by the Philistines, lest they also
should turn traitors on the field. Thus he left the camp
with a greatly increased following. Here, too, was a proof
of God's tender thoughtfulness, because at no time of his
life was he in greater need of reinforcements than now.
God anticipates coming trial, and reinforces us against its
certain imminence and pressure. We are taken into the
House Beautiful to be armed before we descend into the
valley of conflict with Apollyon.

It was altogether according to God's merciful providence that, contrary to his wont, David had left no men to defend Ziklag during his absence. It is difficult to understand the laxity of his arrangements for its safeguard in those wild and perilous times; but apparently not one single soldier was left to protect the women and children. Yet it was well; for when a band of Amalekites fell suddenly on the little town, there was none to irritate them by offering resistance, none to obstruct their will, nothing to excite their fear of pursuit or revenge. Evidently neither David nor his soldiers would be back from the war for weeks or months; there was therefore no need to exercise the usual precautions—they could spread themselves abroad over all the ground, eating and drinking and feasting.

In the first outburst of grief and horror nothing but the gracious interposition of God could have saved David's life. On reaching the spot which they accounted home, after three days' exhausting march, the soldiers found it a heap of smoldering ruins; and instead of the welcome of wives and children, silence and desolation reigned supreme. "Then David and the people that were with him lifted up their voice and wept, until they had no more power to weep;" but in David's case there was an added element of distress. Those who had a little before cried, "Peace, peace to thee, thou son of Jesse; thy God helpeth thee," now spoke of stoning him. The loyalty and devotion which he had never failed to receive from his followers were suddenly changed to vinegar and gall. The milk of human kindness had turned sour in this awful thunderstorm.

But this was the moment of his return to God. In that dread hour, with the charred embers smoking at his feet; with the cold hand of anxiety for the fate of his wives feeling at his heart; with the sense of duplicity and deceit

which he had been practising, and which had alienated him
from God, on his conscience; with this threat of stoning in
his ears, his heart suddenly sprang back into its old resting-
place in the bosom of God. " David was greatly distressed;
for the people spake of stoning him, because the soul of all
the people was grieved, every man for his sons and for his
daughters: *but David strengthened himself in the Lord his
God.*"

From this moment David was himself again, his old
strong, glad, noble self. For the first time, after months
of disuse, he bids Abiathar bring him the ephod, and he
inquires of the Lord. With marvelous vigor he arises to
pursue the marauding troop, and he overtakes it. He
withholds the impetuosity of his men till daylight wanes,
loosing them from the leash in the twilight, and leading
them to the work of rescue and vengeance with such irresistible impetuosity that not a man of them escaped, save
four hundred young men who rode upon camels and fled.
And when the greed of his followers proposed to withhold
from those whose faintness had stayed them by the brook
Besor all share in the rich plunder, he dared to stand alone
against the whole of them, and insisted that it should not
be so, but that as his share was that went down to the
battle, so his should be that tarried by the stuff. Thus he
who had power with God had power also with man.

And when, shortly after, the breathless messenger burst
into his presence with the tidings of Gilboa's fatal rout,
though they meant the fulfilment of long-delayed hopes, he
was able to bear himself humbly and with unaffected sorrow,
to express his lament in the most exquisite funeral ode in
existence, and to award the Amalekite his deserts.

He was sweet as well as strong, as courteous as brave;
for when he returned to Ziklag his first act was to send of
the spoil taken from the Amalekites to the elders of all the

towns on the southern frontier where he and his men were wont to haunt, acknowledging his indebtedness to them, and so far as possible requiting it.

Thus the sunshine of God's favor rested afresh upon his soul. He had broken from Doubting Castle and Giant Despair, and had reached again the path of obedience and safety. God had brought him up from the horrible pit and the miry clay, and set his feet on a rock, and established his goings; and had put a new song of praise in his mouth. Let all backsliders give heed and take comfort. These things were written aforetime for our instruction, that we, through the comfort and instruction of the Scriptures, might have hope.

XIX

𝔗𝔥𝔯𝔦𝔠𝔢 𝔆𝔯𝔬𝔴𝔫𝔢𝔡

(2 SAMUEL i.–iv.)

'For life, with all it yields of joy and woe,
Is just our chance o' the prize of learning love;
And that we hold henceforth to the uttermost
Such prize, despite the envy of the world."

R. BROWNING.

TWO whole days had passed since that triumphant march back from the slaughter of Amalek to the charred and blackened ruins of Ziklag, and it appeared as though David were awaiting some sign to determine his future course. What should he do next? Should he begin to build again the ruined city? Or was there something else on the divine program of his life? His heart was on the watch. He could not forget that when, but a few days back, he had left the camp of Achish, a battle was imminent between the Philistines and his countrymen. Had that battle been fought? And, if so, what had been the issue? How had sped the fortunes of that momentous day? What tidings were there of Saul, of the beloved Jonathan, and of his comrades? Surely it could not be long ere rumors, breathed as on the wind, would answer the questions which were surging through his mind.

On the third day a young man rushed breathless into the camp, his clothes rent, and earth upon his head. He made

straight for David, and fell to the ground at his feet. In
a moment more his tidings were told, each word stabbing
David to the quick. Israel had fled before the foe; large
numbers were fallen on the battle-field; Saul and Jonathan
were dead also. That moment David knew that the
thunder-cloud which had been so long lowering over his
head had broken, and that the expectations of years were
on the point of being realized; but he had no thought for
himself or for the marvelous change in his fortunes. His
generous soul, oblivious to itself, poured out a flood of the
noblest tears man ever shed for Saul, and for Jonathan his
son, and for the people of the Lord, and for the house of
Israel, because they were fallen by the sword.

I. DAVID'S TREATMENT OF SAUL'S MEMORY.—There
could be no doubt that he was dead. His crown, the
symbol of kingly power, and the bracelet worn upon his
arm, were already in David's possession. The Amalekite,
indeed, to lay David more absolutely under obligation, had
made it appear that the king's life had been taken, at his
own request, by himself. "He said to me," so the man's
tale ran, "Stand, I pray thee, beside me, and slay me: for
anguish hath taken hold of me, because my life is yet
whole in me. So I stood beside him, and slew him, because I was sure that he could not live after that he was
fallen." David seems to have been as one stunned till the
evening, and then he aroused himself to show respect to
Saul's memory.

He gave short shrift to the Amalekite. The bearer of the
sad news had been held under arrest, because on his own
showing he had slain the Lord's anointed; and, as the
evening fell, the wretched man was again brought into the
chieftain's presence. David seems to have had some doubt
as to his tale, and it afterward appeared that the story

was false; still it was necessary that the regicide should pay the extreme penalty for the deed to which he had confessed.

With that reverence for the Lord's anointed which had smitten him to the heart when he cut off the piece of his robe, David asked, an expression of horror in his tone, "How wast thou not afraid to put forth thine hand to destroy the Lord's anointed?" Then, calling one of the young men, he bade him go near and fall upon him. And he smote him that he died.

He next poured out his grief in the "Song of the Bow," which at first was taught to and sung by the children of Judah, and has since passed into the literature of the world as an unrivaled model of a funeral dirge. The Dead March in "Saul" is a familiar strain in every national mourning. It was originally called the "Song of the Bow" (verse 18, R.V.), because of the reference to that weapon in the poem.

The greatness of Israel's loss is brought out in the fancied exultation with which the daughters of Philistia would welcome their returning warriors; in the lasting curse invoked on the mountains where the shield of the mighty was polluted with gore and dust; and in the exploits which the heroes wrought with bow and sword before they fell. And then the psalmist bursts into pathetic reminiscences of the ancient friendship which had bound him to the departed. He forgets all he had suffered at the hands of Saul; he thinks only of the ideal of his early manhood. His chivalrous love refuses to consider anything but what had been brave and fair and noble in his liege lord, before self-will had dragged down his soul into the murky abyss, in which for the last few years it had been entombed as in a living grave. "Lovely and pleasant"—such is the epitaph he inscribes on the memorial cenotaph.

But for Jonathan there must be a special stanza. Might

had been his, as Saul's. Had he not, single-handed,
attacked an army and wrought a great deliverance? But
with all his strength he had been sweet. A brother soul,
every memory of whom was very pleasant, like a sweet
strain of music, or the scent of the spring breeze. Tender,
gentle, loving as a woman. A knightly nature; dreaded
by foe, dearly loved by friend; terrible as a whirlwind in
battle, but capable of exerting all the witchery of a woman's
love, and more.

> " Thy love to me was wonderful,
> Passing the love of women."

*Moreover, he sent a message of thanks and congratulation
to the men of Jabesh-gilead.* The indignity with which the
Philistines had treated the royal bodies had been amply ex-
piated by the devotion of the men of Jabesh-gilead. They
had not forgotten that Saul's first act as king had been to
deliver them from a horrible fate. They had organized an
expedition which had taken the bodies of Saul and his three
sons from the walls of Bethshan, to which, after being be-
headed, they were affixed; and had carried them through
the night to their own city, where they had burned them to
save them from further dishonor—the ashes being reverently
buried under the tamarisk-tree in Gilead.

As soon as David heard of this act he sent messengers to
the men of Jabesh-gilead, thanking them for their chivalrous devotion to the memory of the fallen king, and promis-
ing to requite the kindness as one done to the entire nation
and to himself.

In all this David evinced great magnanimity. There
was no thought of himself or his own interests. He had
learned the secret of escaping from himself in his devotion
and care for another. It is the secret of all self-oblivion.
Live in another's life, especially in the interests of your

Master, Christ, and you will be freed from the constant obtrusion and tyranny of self.

II. DAVID'S ATTITUDE WITH RESPECT TO THE KING-DOM.—There is something very beautiful in his movements at this juncture, evidencing how completely his soul had come back to its equipoise in God. He had resumed his old attitude of waiting only upon God, and directing all his expectation to him. It was for God to give him the kingdom, and therefore he refused to take one step toward the throne apart from the direct divine impulse.

This was the more remarkable when so many reasons might have been alleged for immediate action. The kingdom was overrun by Philistines; indeed, it is probable that for the next five years there was no settled government among the northern tribes. It must have been difficult for his patriot heart to restrain itself from gathering the scattered forces of Israel and flinging himself on the foe. He knew, too, that he was God's designated king, and it would have been only natural for him immediately to step up to the empty throne, assuming the scepter as his right. Possibly none would have disputed a vigorous decisive policy of this sort. Abner might have been outmanœuvered, and have shrunk from setting up Ishbosheth at Mahanaim. So mere human judgment might have reasoned. But David was better advised. Refusing to judge according to the judgment of his eyes, he inquired of the Lord, saying, "Shall I go up into any of the cities of Judah?" And when the divine oracle directed him to proceed to Hebron, he does not appear to have gone there in any sense as king or leader, but settled quietly with his followers among the towns and villages in its vicinity, waiting till the men of Judah came, and by a consentaneous movement owned him king. Then for a second time he was anointed.

Anointed first by Samuel in the secrecy of his father's house, he was now anointed king over his own people; just as the Lord Jesus, of whom he was the great exemplar and type, was anointed first by the banks of the Jordan, and again as the representative of his people, when he ascended for them into the presence of the Father, and was set as King on the holy hill of Zion.

We cannot turn from this second anointing without emphasizing the obvious lesson that at each great crisis of our life, and especially when standing on the threshold of some new and enlarged sphere of service, we should seek and receive a fresh anointing to fit us to fulfil its fresh demands. There should be successive and repeated anointings in our life-history as our opportunities widen out in ever-increasing circles. It is a mistake to be always counting back to an anointing which we have received; we must be anointed with fresh oil. When leaving the school for the college, and again when stepping forth from the college to the first cure of souls; when standing at the altar to become a wife, and again when bending over the cradle of the first babe; when summoned to public office in church or state—each new step should be characterized by a definite waiting on God, that there may be a fresh enduement of power, a recharging of the spirit with his might.

III. The Characteristics of David's Reign in Hebron.—For seven years and six months David was king in Hebron over the house of Judah. He was in the prime of life, thirty years of age, and seems to have given himself to the full enjoyment of the quiet sanctities of home. Sandwiched between two references to the long war that lasted between his house and that of Saul is the record of his wives and the names of his children (iii. 2–5).

Throughout those years he preserved that same spirit of

waiting expectancy which was the habit and temper of his
soul, and which was so rarely broken in upon.   In this he
reminds us of our Lord, who sits at his Father's side till his
foes are made the footstool of his feet.   Similarly, David
sat on the throne of Judah, in the city of Hebron—which
means *fellowship*—waiting until God had leveled all difficulties, removed all obstacles, and smoothed the pathway
to the supreme dignity which he had promised.   The only
exception to this policy was his request that Michal should
be restored to him; it would perhaps have been wiser for
them both if she had been left to the husband who seemed
really to love her.   But David may have felt it right to insist on his legal status as the son-in-law of the late king,
and as identified by marriage with the royal house.

With this exception he maintained an almost passive
policy; what fighting was necessary was left to Joab.   The
overtures for the transference of the kingdom of Israel were
finally made by Abner himself, who for years had known
that he was fighting against God, and at last told the
puppet king whom he had set up and supported that what
God had sworn to David he was resolved to effect—
namely, to translate the kingdom from Dan even to
Beersheba, from the house of Saul to that of David.   The
negotiations with Israel and Benjamin were carried out by
Abner in entire independence of David; it was he who had
communications with the elders of Israel, and spake in the
ears of Benjamin, and went finally to speak in the ears of
David in Hebron all that seemed good to Israel and to the
whole house of Benjamin.   It was Abner who proposed to
David to go and gather all Israel unto him, addressing him
as lord and king, and bidding him prepare to rule over all
that his soul desired (iii. 17–21).

Throughout these transactions David quietly receives
what is offered, and only asserts himself with intensity and

passion on two occasions, when it was necessary to clear himself of complicity in dastardly crimes, and to show his detestation and abhorrence of those who had perpetrated them.

It was a noble spectacle when the king followed the bier of Abner and wept at his grave. He forgot that this man had been his persistent foe, and remembered him only as a prince and a great man; and he wove a chaplet of elegiacs to lay on his grave, as he had done for Saul's. It is not wonderful that all the people took notice of it, and it pleased them, as whatever the king did pleased the people.

Then followed the dastardly assassination of the puppet king Ishbosheth. His had been a feeble reign throughout. Located at Mahanaim, on the eastern side of Jordan, he had never exercised more than a nominal sovereignty; all his power was due to Abner, and when he was taken away the entire house of cards crumbled to pieces, and the hapless monarch fell under the daggers of traitors. As soon as they bore the tidings to David, bringing his head as ghastly evidence, David turned to the Lord, who had redeemed him from all adversity, and solemnly swore that he would require at their hands the blood of the murdered man. The reward for the tidings borne by the Amalekite who asserted he had taken Saul's life was death; and surely nothing less could be the sentence on wicked men who had slain a righteous man in his own house, upon his bed.

Then came all the tribes of Israel to that " long stone town on the western slope of the bare terraced hill," and offered him the crown of the entire kingdom. They remembered his kinship with them as their bone and flesh; recalled his former services, when, even in Saul's days, he led out and brought in their armies; and reminded him of the divine promise that he should be shepherd and prince. Then David made a covenant with them, and became their con-

stitutional king, and was solemnly anointed for the third
time; king over the entire people—as the Son of man shall
be one day acknowledged King over the world of men, and
shall reign without a rival.

It is to this period that we must attribute the Eighteenth
Psalm, which undoubtedly touches the high-water mark of
rapturous thankfulness and adoration.   Every precious
name for God is laid under contribution; the figure of his
coming to rescue his servant in a thunder-storm is unparalleled in sublimity.   We can hear the rattle of the hail-
stones, and see the lightning flash, and the gleam of the
coals of fire; and there is throughout an appreciation of
the tenderness and love of God's dealings with his children,
which might have been written by the apostle whom Jesus
loved:

> " Thou hast given me the shield of thy salvation:
> Thy right hand hath holden me up,
> And thy gentleness hath made me great."

XX.

Oh for the Water of the Well of Bethlehem!

(2 SAMUEL v. 17-25; xxi. 15; xxiii. 8.)

" Let us be patient; God has taken from us
   The earthly treasures upon which we leaned,
That from the fleeting things that lie around us
   Our clinging hearts should be forever weaned."

ANNA L. WARING.

IT must have been a rare and imposing assembly that
   came to crown David king of all Israel. The Chronicles record the names and numbers of the principal contingents that were present on that memorable occasion
(1 Chron. xii. 23, etc.). Mighty men of valor from Judah
and Simeon; Levites, led by Jehoiada and Zadok; famous
men from Ephraim; men of Issachar that had understanding of the times; of Zebulun, such as were not of double
heart, and could order the battle array. These and many
more came with a perfect heart to Hebron to make David
king over all Israel. For three days they remained with
him, keeping high festival, the provisions being contributed
by such distant tribes as Zebulun and Naphtali, as well as
by those near at hand, so that all Israel participated in the
joy of the occasion.

The Philistines, however, were watching the scene with
profound dissatisfaction. So long as David was content to
rule as a petty king in Hebron, leaving them free to raid

the northern tribes at their will, they were not disposed to interfere; but when they heard that they had anointed David king over all Israel, all the Philistines went down to seek David.   They probably waited until the august ceremonial was over, and the thousands of Israel had dispersed to their homes, and then poured over into Judah in such vast numbers—spreading themselves in the valley of Ephraim, and cutting off David's connection with the northern tribes—that he was forced to retire with his mighty men and faithful six hundred to the hold, which, by comparison of passages, must have been the celebrated fortress-cave of Adullam (2 Sam. v. 17; xxiii. 13, 14).

I. A Sudden Reversal of Fortune.—It was but as yesterday that David was the center of the greatest assembly of warriors that his land had seen for many generations. With national acclaim he had been carried to the throne of a united people.   He realized that he was fondly enshrined in the hearts of his countrymen.   But to-day he is driven from Hebron, where for more than seven years he had dwelt in undisturbed security, back to that desolate mountain fastness in which years before he had taken refuge from the hatred of Saul.   It was a startling reversal of fortune, a sudden overcasting of a radiant noon, a bolt out of a clear sky.   It is probable, however, that he took refuge in God.   These were days when he walked very closely with his almighty Friend, and he did not for a moment waver in his confidence that God would perfect what concerned him, and establish him firmly in his kingdom.

REVERSALS CAN BE GOOD TOO!
9-17-2002

Such sudden reversals come to us all—to wean us from confidence in men and things; to stay us from building our nest on any earth-grown tree; to force us to root ourselves in God alone.   It was salutary that David should be re-

minded at this crisis of his history that he was as dependent
on God as ever, and that he who had given could as easily
take back his gifts.   Child of mortality, such lessons will
inevitably be set before thee to learn.   In the hour of
most radiant triumphs thou must remember Him who has
accounted thee fit to be his steward; thou must understand
that thy place and power are thine only as his gift, and as
a trusteeship for his glory.   Be not surprised, then, if he
makes thy throne tremble now and again, that thou mayest
remember that it rests, not on some inherent necessity, but
only on the determination of his will, the forth-putting of
his might.

This contrast between the anointing of Hebron and the
conflict of Adullam presents a striking analogy to the experiences of our Lord, who, after his anointing at the banks
of the Jordan, was driven by the Spirit into the wilderness
of Judæa to be forty days tempted of the devil.   It is the
law of the spiritual life.   The bright life of popularity is
too strong and searching for the perfect development of
the divine life.   Loneliness, solitude, temptation, conflict
—these are the flames that burn the divine colors into
the character; such the processes through which the blessings of our anointing are made available for the poor, the
broken-hearted, the prisoners, the captives, and the blind.

II. GLEAMS OF LIGHT.—The misty gloom of these dark
hours was lit by some notable incidents.   The mighty men
excelled themselves in single combats with the Philistine
champions.   Then Abishai, the son of Zeruiah, smote the
giant who with his new sword thought to have slain
David; and Elhanan slew the brother of Goliath of Gath;
and Jonathan, David's nephew, slew a huge monstrosity
who had defied Israel; and Eleazar stood in the breach,
when the rest had fled, and smote the Philistines till his

hand was weary, and the discomfited soldiers returned only to spoil. Such prodigies of valor were performed around the person of their prince, whom his followers delighted to call the Light of Israel, albeit for the hour obscured by clinging mists (xxi. 17).

What marvels may be wrought by the inspiration of a single life! We cannot but revert in thought to that hour when, hard by that very spot, an unknown youth stepped forth from the affrighted hosts of Israel to face the dreaded Goliath. Alone, so far as human succor went, he had encountered and defeated that terrible antagonist; but now, after some fourteen or fifteen years had run their course, he no longer stood by himself; there were scores of men, animated by his spirit, inspired by his faith, who pushed him gently back, and told him that they must be permitted to bear the brunt of the conflict, since his life, which was the fountain-source of all their energy, must be carefully withheld from needless peril.

Thus the lives of great men light up and inspire other lives. They mold their contemporaries. The inspiration of a Wesley's career raises a great army of preachers. The enthusiasm of a Carey, a Livingstone, a Paton, stirs multitudes of hearts with missionary zeal. Those who had been the disciples of Jesus became his apostles and martyrs. His own life of self-sacrifice for men has become the beacon-fire that has summoned myriads from the lowland valley of selfishness to the surrender, the self-denial, the anguish of the cross, if only they might follow in his steps.

III. A Touching Incident.—Adullam was not far from Bethlehem. Often, in his earliest years, David had led his father's flocks to pasture amid the valleys where he was now sheltering; and the familiar scenes recalled, as a scent or strain is wont to do, memories which came trooping back from the past, and spoke to him of Jesse and his mother and his boyhood's home.

One sultry afternoon, as it would seem, these recollections were unusually fresh and vivid. He was a semi-prisoner in the hold. Over yonder, almost within sight, a garrison of Philistines held Bethlehem. Suddenly an irresistible longing swept across him to taste the water of the well of Bethlehem, which was by the gate. Almost involuntarily he gave expression to the wish. He did not suspect that any of his stalwarts were within earshot, or, if there were, that they would be foolhardy enough to attempt to gratify his whim. If he had thought this, however, he miscalculated. He had not gauged the warmth of the affection with which those strong men loved him.

Three of his mightiest warriors overheard their chieftain's wish, stole secretly out of the cave and down the valley, burst through the host of the Philistines, drew water from the well, and, before they had been missed, placed the brimming vessel in David's hands. It was the priceless expression of a love that was stronger than death. He could not drink it. To him the vessel seemed gleaming crimson with the blood it might have cost. With that instinctive chivalry of soul which made him in all the changes of his fortune so absolutely kingly as to compel the enthusiastic devotion of his adherents, he arose and poured it out as a libation to God, as though the gift were fit only to be made to him; saying, as he did so, " My God forbid it me, that I should do this : shall I drink the blood of these men that have put their lives in jeopardy? "

We have another example in this graphic episode of David's marvelous self-control. Up to this time of his life he seems always to have lived with the tightly girded loin —no desire was allowed to have unchallenged sway. The wayward impulse of passion, the assertion of caprice, were repressed by the iron determination of the purpose in all things to live according to the loftiest ideals of manhood and kingliness. The question of selfish gratification was always secondary to the considerations of high and noble principle.

It were well if all young men and women—aye, and others also—who read these words would ask themselves whether certain gratifications in which they, with others of their class, have been accustomed to indulge are not purchased at too dear a cost. Could they quaff the cup of pleasure in the theater and opera-house if they realized that it was presented to their lips at the cost of scores of souls, whose modesty and virtue were being sacrificed behind the scenes? Could they drink of the intoxicating cup, as a beverage, if they realized that the drinking customs of society were annually costing the happiness, the life, and the eternal welfare of myriads?

How often we sigh for the waters of the well of Bethlehem! We go back on our past, and dwell longingly on never-to-be-forgotten memories. Oh to see again that face; to feel the touch of that gentle hand; to hear that voice! Oh to be again as in those guileless happy years, when the forbidden fruit had never been tasted, and the flaming sword had never been passed! Oh for that fresh vision of life, that devotion to the Saviour's service, that new glad outburst of love! Oh that one would give us to drink of the water of the well of Bethlehem, which is beside the gate! They are vain regrets; there are no mighties strong enough to break through the serried ranks of the years and fetch back the past. But the quest of the soul may yet be satisfied by what awaits it in Him who said, "He that drinketh of this water shall thirst again: but he that drinketh of the water that I shall give him shall never thirst; but it shall be in him a spring of water rising up to everlasting life." Not in Bethlehem's well, but in Him who was born there, shall the soul's thirst be quenched forever.

IV. THE OVERTHROW OF THE PHILISTINES.—Prosperity had not altered the attitude of David's soul in its persistent waiting on God. As he was when first he came to Hebron, so he was still; and in this hour of perplexity he inquired of the Lord, saying, "Shall I go up against the Philistines? wilt thou deliver them into mine hand?" In reply he received the divine assurance of certain victory; and when the battle commenced it seemed to him as if the Lord himself were sweeping them before him like a winter flood, which, rushing down the mountain-side, carries all before it in its impetuous rush. "The Lord," said he, "hath broken forth upon mine enemies." The routed foe had no time even to gather up their gods, which fell into the conqueror's hands.

Again the Philistines came up to assert their olden supremacy, and again David waited on the Lord for direction. It was well that he did so, because the plan of campaign was not as before. Those that rely on God's coöperation must be careful to be in constant touch with him. The aid which was given yesterday in one form will be given to-morrow in another. In the first battle the position of the Philistines was carried by assault; in the second it was turned by ambush. To have reversed the order, or to have acted on the two occasions identically, would have missed the method and movement of those divine legions who acted as David's invincible allies.

This movement in the mulberry-trees, which indicated that the ambush must bestir itself and advance on the foe, suggests the footfalls of invisible angelic squadrons passing

onward to the battle. " The Lord is gone out before thee
to smite the host of the Philistines." Then David broke on
their ranks and pursued them from Gibeon unto the heart
of the maritime plain.

Sometimes we have to march, sometimes to halt; now
we are called to action, again to suffering; in this battle to
rush forward like a torrent, in the next to glide stealthily to
ambush and wait. We must admit nothing stereotyped in
our methods. What did very well in the house of Dorcas
will not suit in the stately palace of Cornelius. Let there
be living faith in God; the calm waiting on the housetop
in prayer; the perception of the new departure which the
Spirit of God is intending and foreshadowing; and the
willingness to follow, though it be at the sacrifice of all the
older prejudices. Then shall we know what God can do
as a mighty coöperating force in our lives, making a breach
in our foes, and marching his swift-stepping legions to our
succor.

XXI

Ierusalem, the Holy City

(2 SAMUEL v.)

" Fair Jerusalem,
The Holy City, lifted high her towers."
MILTON, *Paradise Regained.*

ONE of the first acts of the new king was to secure a suitable capital for his kingdom. And his choice of Jerusalem was a masterpiece of policy and statesmanship. Surely it was more; it was the result of the direct guidance of the Spirit of God. This was the time of which Jehovah speaks in that passage of Ezekiel: "I passed by thee, and looked upon thee; behold, thy time was the time of love; and I swore unto thee, and entered into a covenant with thee, and thou becamest mine" (xvi. 8).

It was highly desirable that the capital should be accessible to the whole country, and should possess the necessary features that rendered it fit to become the heart and brain of the national life. It must be capable of being strongly fortified, so as to preserve the sacred treasures of the kingdom inviolate. It must combine features of strength and beauty, so as to arouse the national pride and devotion. It must be hallowed by sacred associations, so as to become the religious center of the people's holiest life. All these features blended in Jerusalem, and commended it to David's divinely guided judgment. In this he greatly differed from Saul, who had made his own city, Gibeah, his capital—an altogether insignificant place, and the scene of an atrocious crime, the infamy of which could not be obliterated. To have made Hebron the capital would have excited the jealousy of the rest of Israel; and Bethlehem, his birthplace, would have struck too low a key-note. None were to be compared with the site of Jerusalem, on the frontier between Judah and Benjamin, surrounded on three sides by valleys, and on the other side, the north, strongly fortified.

I. ITS PREVIOUS HISTORY.—To the Jew there was no city like Jerusalem. It was the city of his God, situate in his holy mountain : " Beautiful in elevation, the joy of the whole earth." The high hills of Bashan were represented as jealous of the lowlier hill of Zion, because God had chosen it for his abode. The mountains that stood around her seemed to symbolize the environing presence of Jehovah. The exile in his banishment opened his windows toward Jerusalem as he knelt in prayer, and wished that his right hand might forget its cunning sooner than his heart fail to prefer Jerusalem above its chief joy. The charm of the yearly pilgrimage to the sacred feasts was that the feet of the pilgrim should stand within her gates; and when at a distance from her walls and palaces, pious hearts were wont to pray that peace and prosperity might be within them for the sake of those brethren and companions who were favored to live within her precincts. The noblest bosom that ever throbbed with true human emotion heaved with convulsive sobs at the thought of the desolation impending over her. Jesus wept when he beheld the city, and said, " O Jerusalem, Jerusalem, how often would I have gathered thee, as a hen gathers her chickens beneath her wings, and ye would not ! "

But it had not always been so. Her birth and nativity
were of the land of the Canaanite. An Amorite was her
father, and her mother a Hittite. In the day that she was
born she was cast out as a deserted child on the open field,
weltering in her blood. For a brief spell the priest-king
Melchizedek reigned over her, and during his life her future
glory must have been presaged: the thin spiral columns of
smoke that arose from his altars anticipating the stately
worship of the temple; his priesthood foreshadowing a
long succession of priests. Thereafter a long spell of darkness befell her; and for years after the rest of the country
was in occupation of Israel, Jerusalem was still held by the
Jebusites. Joshua, indeed, nominally subdued the city in
his first occupation of the land, and slew its king; but his
tenure of it was very brief and slight, and the city speedily
relapsed under the sway of its ancient occupants.

II. THE CAPTURE.—Making a levy of all Israel, David
went up to Jerusalem. For the first time after seven years
he took the lead of his army in person. Passive when he
was called to wait for the gift of God, he was intensely ac-
tive and energetic when he discerned the divine summons.
The Jebusites ridiculed the attempt to dislodge them.
They had held the fortress for so long, and were so confident of its impregnable walls, that in derision they placed
along the walls a number of cripples, and boasted that these
would be strong enough to keep David and his whole army
at bay. But it appears from the narrative given by
Josephus that Joab, incited by David's proclamation of
making the captor of the city his commander-in-chief,
broke in by a subterranean passage excavated in the soft
limestone rock, made his way into the very heart of the
citadel, and opened the gates to the entire army.

Whether this story be true or not, it is certain that

through Joab's prowess the city speedily fell into David's hands; and he dwelt in the stronghold afterward known as Zion, or the city of David. This was only part of what was afterward known as Jerusalem. Moriah, where afterward the temple was erected, was probably an unoccupied site. Araunah the Jebusite had a threshing-floor there.

David's first act was to extend the fortifications: "He built round about from Millo and inward;" while Joab seems to have repaired and beautified the buildings in the city itself. This first success laid the foundation of David's greatness. "He waxed greater and greater; for the Lord, the God of hosts, was with him." Indeed, neighboring nations appear to have become impressed with the growing strength of his kingdom, and hastened to seek his alliance (1 Chron. xi. 7–9; 2 Sam. v. 11).

III. A Fair Dawn.—It has been suggested that we owe the One Hundred and First Psalm to this hour in David's life. He finds himself suddenly called to conduct the internal administration of a great nation, that had, so to speak, been born in a day, and was beginning to throb with the intensity of a long-suspended animation. The new needs were demanding new expression. Departments of law and justice, of finance and of military organization, were rapidly being called into existence, and becoming localized at the capital. Functionaries and officials of every description were being created. The palace and court were every day thronged with those who sought promotion to offices of trust. It was highly desirable that no mistake should be made in these early selections, and that the country should be reassured as to the character of the men whom the king was prepared to intrust with its concerns. For these purposes this psalm may have been prepared. In any case, it exactly suits such an occasion and purpose.

The royal psalmist declares that he will behave himself wisely in a perfect way, and will walk within his house with a perfect heart. He will set no base thing before his eyes, and hate the work of those that turn aside. Then he describes those who shall be his chosen councilors and ministers. He will listen to no privy slanders, subtly suggested to his ear, as from another Doeg or Cush. He will not suffer Hamans, with their high looks and proud hearts, to rule his privy council and oppress the poor Mordecais at the gate. If he discovers deceit or falsehood in any of his attendants, any species of deception or misrepresentation, he pledges himself to dismiss him instantly. His earliest and best energies should be devoted to cutting off all workers of iniquity from the city of the Lord, and to the destruction of all the wicked of the land; while his eyes should be upon all the faithful of the land, *they* should dwell with him, and he would choose as his most favored attendants those who walked in a perfect way.

It was a fair ideal. These early days of the new kingdom were fitly described by him, as he reviewed them from the threshold of eternity, as a morning without clouds, or as when the tender grass springeth out of the earth through clear shining after rain. The conception of the righteous ruler, ruling men in the fear of God, and thrusting away the ungodly as thorns and briers, stood out sharply defined and clear-cut before him. It beckoned to him to follow, and if only he had obeyed and followed, without swerving to the right or left, what tears of blood, what years of anguish, would have been saved! As a dying man, that ideal of more than thirty years before came back on him, and compared sadly with what had actually befallen him. It was bitter to contrast what had been with what might have been; the muddy swamp in which the river of his life had nearly lost itself with the clear crystal of its first inception (2 Sam. xxiii. 1–5).

XXII

The Conveyance of the Ark to Mount Zion

(2 SAMUEL vi.)

" Hark! what a sound, and too divine for hearing,
  Stirs on the earth, and trembles in the air!
Is it the thunder of the Lord's appearing?
  Is it the music of his people's prayer?
Surely he cometh! and a thousand voices
  Shout to the saints, and to the deaf are dumb!
Surely he cometh! and the earth rejoices,
  Glad in his coming, who hath sworn, ' I come.' "

F. MYERS.

AS soon as David had acquired a capital he was eager to
make it the religious, as well as the political, center
of the national life.   With this object in view, he resolved
to place in a temporary structure hard by his palace the
almost forgotten ark; which, since its return from the land
of the Philistines, had found a temporary resting-place in
the "city of the woods," some eleven miles southwest of
Jerusalem, in the house and under the care of Abinadab.

In all probability David felt unable to remove the tabernacle—which, after Saul's slaughter of the priests, had
been set up in the high place that was at Gibeon—because
Zadok the priest, and his brethren the priests, ministered to
it, and maintained the burnt-offering continually upon the
altar.   An old root of jealousy lay between the families of
Zadok and Abiathar; and it was wiser in every way not to

bring them together, or to interfere with the religious rites which had been maintained through the broken years of recent history (1 Chron. xvi. 39, etc.). But David's purpose would be sufficiently served by securing the presence of the ark in the heart of the new city. He would not, however, take any step upon his own initiative, but consulted with the captains of thousands and of hundreds, even with every leader. With their acquiescence he sent abroad everywhere throughout all the land of Israel to gather priests, Levites, and people, to bring again the sacred emblem.

I. THE MISTAKE OF THE CART.—It was a great procession that wended its way that day to the little town. In addition to a vast host of priests and Levites, and a great concourse of people, there were thirty thousand chosen soldiers, whose presence would be sufficient to protect the assembly from any hostile incursion or surprise.

Probably we owe the One Hundred and Thirty-second Psalm to this occasion, in which the royal singer records the determination which he had formed in the days of his affliction, that whenever he should be delivered from them, and established in his kingdom, one of his earnest acts would be to find out a place for the Lord, a tabernacle for the Mighty One of Jacob. Then follow the magnificent stanzas which refer directly to this event:

> " Lo, we heard of it in Ephratah:
> We found it in Kirjath-jearim.
> We will go into his tabernacles:
> We will worship at his footstool.
> Arise, O Lord, into thy resting-place;
> Thou, and the ark of thy strength."

But one fatal mistake marred the events of the day, and postponed the fulfilment of the nation's high hope and resolve. It was strictly ordained in the law of Moses that Levites alone, specially consecrated to the task, should bear the ark upon their shoulders, not touching it with their hands, lest they should die (Num. iv. 15 ; vii. 9). Nothing could be clearer than this specific injunction, or more obvious than the reason for it, in enforcing the sanctity of all that pertained to the service of the Most High. This command had, however, fallen into disuse with much else ; and it was arranged that the ark should be carried on a new cart driven by the two sons of Abinadab. This mistake could not be passed over. That the Philistines had used such a cart with impunity had been permitted because they did it ignorantly; but for Israel to set aside the repeated injunction of the Levitical law, and follow their own caprice, could not be condoned, lest the entire Levitical code should be treated as a dead letter and sink into desuetude.

The oxen started amid a blast of song and trumpet, and for the first two miles all went well, until they came upon a piece of rough road, on which the oxen stumbled, and the ark shook so violently as to be in danger of being precipitated to the ground. Then Uzzah, the younger son of Abinadab, who perhaps had become too familiar with the sacred emblem, put out his hand to steady it, and instantly fell dead. The effect on the procession was terrific. Horror silenced the song, and panic spread through the awed crowd as the tidings of the catastrophe spread backward through its ranks. David was greatly dismayed. He was afraid of God that day, and said, "How shall I bring the ark of God home to me ?" So he directed that the ark should be deposited in the house of Obed-edom, a Levite, who lived in the vicinity, and there it remained for three months. The terrified crowds returned to Jerusalem in consternation and dismay.

It has been suggested in some quarters that the breach
of Uzzah was a needlessly severe act of God—a too stern
treatment of a sin of ignorance.   On the other hand, it
must be borne in mind how important it was at this juncture to insist on literal obedience to the ancient code.   If
it had been permitted to man's caprice to set its injunctions
at defiance, it is easy to see that the entire system might
have fallen into disuse, and its important functions been
left unrealized.

II. The Shoulders of Living Men.—"The Lord
blessed the home of Obed-edom."   Josephus states that
from the moment the ark rested beneath his roof, a tide
of golden prosperity set in, so that he passed from poverty
to wealth; an evident sign that Jehovah had no contro-
versy with those who obeyed the regulations and conditions
laid down in the ancient law.   In the meanwhile David
searched into the divine directions for the conveyance of
the sacred emblem; for he said, "None ought to carry the
ark of the Lord but Levites: for them hath the Lord
chosen to carry the ark of God, and to minister unto him
forever."

Again a vast concourse was gathered.   This time, however, the prescribed ritual was minutely observed; and the
children of the Levites bare the ark of God upon their
shoulders, with the staves thereon, as Moses commanded,
according to the word of the Lord.   Then the deep bass
of the white-robed choirs, the clash of the cymbals of brass,
the sweet strains of the bands of psalteries and harps, the
measured march of the captains over thousands, the stately
procession of the elders, the shoutings of the teeming crowds
of all Israel, together made up such a welcome as was
worthy of the occasion, and thrilled the soul of David, re-

sponsive as a musical instrument to a master hand. Clad
in a linen ephod, he leaped and danced before the Lord.

So they brought in the ark of the Lord, and set it in its
place, in the midst of the tent that David had pitched for
it; and David offered burnt-offerings and peace-offerings
before the Lord. Then he turned to bless the people in
the name of the Lord of hosts, and distributed to them
bread and wine and raisins. The one cloud that marred
the gladness of the day was the biting speech of Michal,
who had no sympathy with her husband's religion. Poor
woman! perhaps she was still smarting over the loss of
Phaltiel; possibly she was jealous at David's independence
of her and her father's house—hence the venom in her
speech to the man whom she had loved, and whose life she
had once saved.

III. THREE MAJESTIC PSALMS.—Upon this occasion
three of the greatest psalms were composed—the Fifteenth,
Sixty-eighth, and Twenty-fourth. The Fifteenth Psalm
was evidently composed with direct reference to the death
of Uzzah, and in answer to the question:

> " Lord, who shall sojourn in thy tabernacle?
> Who shall dwell in thy holy hill? "

The Sixty-eighth Psalm was chanted as a processional
hymn. It begins with the ancient formula uttered in the
desert march each time the camp was struck:

> " Let God arise, let his enemies be scattered:
> Let them also that hate him flee before him."

As the ark was borne forward in its majestic progress,
the symphony was softly played which told of the ancient
days in which He went before his people and marched

through the wilderness, while the earth trembled and the heavens dropped at his presence.

As the Levite bearers drew near the ascent of the road up to the citadel of Zion, the high mountains of Bashan were depicted as regarding its lowlier height with envy; and then, as the august procession swept up the steep, the choristers broke into a strophe of unrivaled grandeur, the full meaning of which could only be fulfilled in the ascension of the Christ himself, far above all principality and power, into the presence of his Father:

" Thou hast ascended on high, thou hast led captivity captive:
  Thou hast received gifts for men,
  Even for the rebellious, that the Lord God might dwell among
    them."

An enumeration of the constituent parts of that mighty host follows: the singers who went before, and the minstrels that followed after; the damsels that played with timbrels, and the great host of women publishing the tidings; little Benjamin and the princes of Judah; the princes of Zebulun and of Naphtali. Finally, the psalmist anticipates the gathering of distant nations to that sacred spot:

" Princes shall come out of Egypt;
  Ethiopia shall haste to stretch out her hands unto God."

But the Twenty-fourth Psalm is perhaps the master ode of the three. It begins with a marvelous conception, when we consider the narrowness of ordinary Jewish exclusiveness:

" The earth is the Lord's, and the fullness thereof;
  The world, and they that dwell therein."

The first half of the psalm answers the question as to the kind of men who may stand before God (vs. 3–6).

They must be clean in hands and pure in heart, not lifting their soul to vanity nor swearing deceitfully. No mere ablutions or external ceremonial will meet the case. The requirement of this holy God is the righteousness which he alone can give to those who seek his face.

The second half declares God's willingness to abide with man upon the earth. The low-browed gates, beneath which Melchizedek may have come forth to greet Abraham, seemed all too low to admit the ark borne aloft on the Levites' shoulders; and they were bidden to lift up themselves and open to the entering King. In thunders of voice and instrument, the white-robed choirs, halting before the closed portals, cried:

> " Lift up your heads, O ye gates ;
> And be ye lifted up, ye everlasting doors;
> And the King of glory shall come in."

Then from within a single voice, as though of some startled and suspicious warder, demands:

> " Who is this King of glory? "

a question which met with the immediate, emphatic, and mighty response:

> " The Lord strong and mighty,
> The Lord mighty in battle."

Again the challenge to open. Again the inquiry.

Again the magnificent reply, that the King of glory—for whom admittance was demanded to this ancient city, held once by demons, the nest of every unclean bird—is the Lord of hosts, to whom all angels, all demons, all the living things in heaven, and on earth, and under the earth, are subject. So the ark at last reached its resting-place.

XXIII

"𝔗𝔥𝔬𝔫 𝔐𝔦𝔡𝔰𝔱 𝔚𝔢𝔩𝔩 𝔱𝔥𝔞𝔱 𝔦𝔱 𝔴𝔞𝔰 𝔦𝔫 𝔱𝔥𝔦𝔫𝔢 𝔥𝔢𝔞𝔯𝔱"

(2 SAMUEL vii. ; 2 CHRONICLES vi. 8.)

> " There lives
> A Judge, who, as man claims by merit, gives;
> To whose all-pondering mind a noble aim,
> Faithfully kept, is as a noble deed;
> In whose pure sight all virtue doth succeed."
> WORDSWORTH.

WITH the assistance of Hiram, king of Tyre, a palace of cedar had been erected for David on Mount Zion. It was a remarkable contrast to the shelter of Adullam's cave, or even to any house he might have occupied during his stay at Hebron. It was a great contrast, also, to the temporary structure which served as a house for the ark. One day the impulse suddenly came to David to realize a purpose the germ-thought of which had probably been long in his heart. Calling Nathan, the prophet, now mentioned for the first time, he announced to him his intention of building a house for God. For the moment the prophet cordially assented to the proposal; but in the quiet of the night, when he was more able to ascertain the thought of God, the word of the Lord came to him, and bade him stay the king from taking further steps in that direction.

The next day he broke the news to David with the utmost delicacy and gentleness. Indeed, in the account of his interview with the king it is difficult to detect the sentence which contained the direct negative. The impression of the whole is that the offer was refused; but the refusal was wrapped up in so many assurances of blessing, in so much promise and benediction, that the king was hardly sensible of disappointment amid the rush of intense and overwhelming gladness which Nathan's words aroused: "Wilt thou build a house for God? He will build thee a house."

I. A CONCEPTION OF A NOBLE PURPOSE ·It was a great thought that came to David. It was in part suggested by the exigencies of the situation. After the ark had come to its new home, Asaph and others had been appointed to celebrate, and thank and praise the Lord, and minister before him (1 Chron. xvi. 4–37); and it is supposed that at this period the twenty-four courses of priests were appointed, an arrangement which lasted to the time of our Lord. It is also supposed that the Levites were now organized—twenty-four thousand to help the priests, four thousand as musicians and singers, four thousand as guards and watchmen; while the remainder were scattered throughout the land to teach the law, execute justice, and perform other public offices. An immense body of men was thus gathering around the ark and palace, for whom it was necessary to find suitable headquarters; and this, no doubt, partly urged David toward the fulfilment of his purpose. But surely there was a deeper reason: to show his love for God; to establish some monument of his reverence, devotion, and lasting gratitude.

It is thus, especially in young life, that great conceptions visit the soul; ideals of surpassing beauty cast a light forward upon the future; resolves of service for God and man brace the soul as the air from the glaciers does the dwellers in the plains; and all life assumes a nobler aspect and is

set to a higher key.   Secretly that lad resolves to be a
preacher, missionary, or philanthropist; and that girl to be
queen in an ideal home, or to go far hence to the zenanas
of India.   " I will do this great thing for God," the young
heart says to itself, altogether heedless of sacrifice, tears,
blood.   The bugle-notes of lofty purpose ring out gladly,
summoning the soul to noble exploit; and it is saved from
the low levels which satisfy others by the immortal hope
that has already gone forward to occupy the future.

Young people, never surrender your ideal, nor act
unworthily of it, nor disobey the heavenly vision.   Above
all, when you come to the house of cedar, and God has
given you rest, be more than ever careful to gird yourselves,
and arise to realize the purpose that visited you when you
kept your father's sheep.

II. The Ideal is not Always Realized.—There is
no definite " No " spoken by God's gentle lips.   He presses
his promises and blessings upon us, and leads us forward
in a golden haze of love, which conceals his negative.
Like David, we can hardly point the word or moment of
refusal; we are lovingly carried forward from sentence to
sentence in life's long speech of divine care and bounty;
and it is only in moments of review that we find that
our purpose is not destined to work itself out just as we
thought.

The plant is conscious of a great possibility throbbing
within it; but somehow the days pass and it does not come
to a flower.   The picture which is to gain immortality is
always *to be* painted; the book which is to elucidate the
problem of the ages is always *to be* written; the immortal
song is always *to be* sung.   The young man is kept at his
desk in the counting-house instead of going to the pulpit;
the girl becomes a withered woman, cherishing a faded

flower; the king hands on to his son the building of the
house.

III. GOD EXPLAINS HIS REASONS AFTERWARD.—What
we know not now, we shall know hereafter.   Years after
David said to Solomon, his son, not born at this time, "The
word of the Lord came to me, saying, Thou hast shed blood
abundantly, and hast made great wars: thou shalt not build
a house unto my name" (1 Chron. xxii. 8).   The blood-
stained hand might not raise the temple of peace.   It
would have wounded David needlessly to have been told
this at the time.   It was enough to wrap up the divine
"No" in a promise of infinite blessing; but, as the years
passed, the reason for God's refusal grew clear and distinct
before him.   Meanwhile David possessed his soul in
patience, and said to himself, "God has a reason; I can
not understand it, but it is well."

Some day we shall understand that God has a reason in
every "No" which he speaks through the slow movement
of life.   He would reveal it to us if we could bear it; but
it is better not to pry into the mystery of his providence
He fences our questions, saying, "If I will that he tarry,
what is that to thee?"   But the time will come, probably
in this life—certainly in the next—when the word of the
Lord will come to us; and from the eminence of the years
we shall descry why he led us as he did.

IV. AN UNREALIZED CONCEPTION MAY YET BE
FRAUGHT WITH IMMENSE BLESSING.—Solomon completes
the story: "The Lord said unto David my father, Whereas
it was in thine heart to build a house for my name, thou
didst well that it was in thine heart."   David was a better
man because he had given expression to the noble purpose.
Its gleam left a permanent glow on his life.   The rejected

candidate to the missionary society stands upon a higher moral platform than those who were never touched by the glow of missionary enthusiasm. For a woman to have loved passionately, even though the dark waters may have ingulfed her love before it was consummated, leaves her ever after richer, deeper, than if she had never loved, nor been loved in return. That a plant should have dreamed in some dark night of the possibility of flowering into matchless beauty stamps it as belonging to a higher family than the moss that clings around the stump. "Thou didst well that it was in thine heart."

The martyrs in the apocalyptic vision behold a day when their wrongs will be avenged; but they are told to wait, since God's time had not come; in the meanwhile white robes are given them. Their ideal was not yet, but it purified them, and bound them closer to the Christ.

God will credit us with what we would have been if we might. He that has the missionary's heart, though he be tied to an office-stool, is reckoned as one of that noble band; the woman at Zarephath, who did nothing more than share her last meal with the prophet, shall have a prophet's reward; the soul that thrills with the loftiest impulses, which the cares of the widowed mother or dependent relatives stay in fulfilment, will be surprised one day to find itself credited with the harvest which would have been reaped had those seed-germs been cast on more propitious soil. In the glory David will find himself credited with the building of the temple on Mount Zion.

V. Do the Next Thing.—The energy which David would have expended in building the temple wrought itself out in gathering the materials for its construction: "I have prepared with all my might for the house of my God . . ." (1 Chron. xxix. 2, etc.). If you cannot have what you hoped, do not sit down in despair and allow the energies of your life to run to waste; but arise, and gird yourself to help others to achieve. If you may not build, you may gather materials for him that shall. If you may not go down the mine, you can hold the ropes.

There is a fact in nature known as the law of the conservation of force. The force of the accumulating velocity of the falling stone passes into heat, of which some is retained by the stone, the rest passes into the atmosphere. No true ideals are fruitless; somehow they help the world of men. No tears are wept, no prayers uttered, no conceptions honestly entertained in vain.

Somehow God makes up to us. He stooped over David's life in blessing. The promise made through Nathan was threefold: (1) that David's house should reign forever; (2) that David's seed should build the temple; (3) that the kingdom of Israel should be made sure. As we read the glowing words we feel that they could only be realized in Him whom Peter declares David foresaw. There was only One of the sons of men whose reign can be permanent, and his kingdom without end; who can bring rest to the weary sons of men, and build the true temple of God (Acts ii. 30). But how great the honor that he should be David's Son!

Then David, the king, went in and sat before the Lord, and he said, "Who am I, O Lord God? . . . " (2 Sam. vii. 18). We have no words to characterize the exuberant outflow of his soul in that transcendent hour. There was no complaint that the purpose of his heart was thwarted amid the successive billows of glory that swept over his soul. Does God withhold the less and not give the greater? Does he refuse the offer we make, and not bestow some heavenly gift that enriches forevermore? Dare to trust him; sit before him, and let his assurances comfort thee.

Claim that he should do as he has said, and know that not
one good thing shall fail: " For brass he will bring gold,
for iron silver, for wood brass, and for stones iron. . . . The
sun shall be no more thy light by day; neither for bright-
ness shall the moon give light unto thee: but the Lord
shall be unto thee an everlasting light, and thy God thy
glory."

XXIV

"𝔜et have 𝔍 𝔖et my 𝔎ing"

(2 SAMUEL viii. ; I CHRONICLES xviii., xix., xx.)

" Crown him the Lord of heaven,
Enthroned in worlds above,
Crown him the King to whom is given
The wondrous name of Love!
Crown him with many crowns,
As thrones before him fall;
Crown him, ye kings, with many crowns,
For he is King of all!"

THE time of rest which succeeded the removal of the
ark was broken in upon by a succession of fierce
wars. One after another the surrounding nations gathered
together, either singly or in confederacies, against David.
"The nations raged, the kingdoms were moved."

The Philistines.—For the last time they arose; but
David smote and subdued them, and, to use the significant
phrase of the Revised Version, took the bridle of the
mother-city out of their hand.

The Moabites.—The hereditary alliance, dating from the
time of Ruth, between the Hebrew monarch and his restless neighbors was insufficient to restrain them; and Benaiah was commissioned to lead an expedition against them,
which was so successful that their entire army fell into his
hands, and was dealt with according to the terrible custom
of the time, one third only being spared.

187

The Syrians.—The king of Zobah and the Syrians of Damascus were utterly defeated; vast spoils of gold and brass fell into David's hand, and the border of Israel was carried to the line of the Euphrates, so that the ancient promise made by God to Abraham was fulfilled: "Unto thy seed have I given this land, from the river of Egypt unto the great river, the river Euphrates."

Edom.—While David was engaged in the north, the Edomites invaded Judah, and Abishai was despatched against them. On the west shore of the Dead Sea he encountered them, and slew eighteen thousand in the Valley of Salt. The whole land, even to Petra, its rock-bound capital, was slowly reduced to submission; and, with the exception of Hadad, who made his way to Egypt, the royal family was exterminated.

Ammon.—A friendly overture on the part of David was met with gross insult; and Hanun, apprehending the infliction of condign revenge, formed a vast coalition. The combined forces amounted to thirty-two thousand, with a strong contingent of cavalry and chariots, against which David could only oppose the Hebrew infantry, the use of horses being forbidden by the Mosaic legislation. It was a supreme moment in David's career, and taxed the utmost resources of Joab's generalship. By God's good hand, however, victory was secured; the tide of Israelite invasion swept over the hostile country; Rabbah, the capital city, fell into David's hand; the people were put to work with saws, arrows, and axes, probably preparing the materials for the erection of public works, and perhaps of the temple itself.

These years of war gave birth to some of the grandest of the psalms, among which may be numbered the Second, Twentieth, Twenty-first, Sixtieth, and One Hundred and Tenth.

I. THE FOE.—The nations rage; the peoples imagine
a vain thing; the kings of the earth set themselves, and the
rulers take counsel together against the Lord, and against
his anointed. We hear their plottings in their council-
chambers:

> " Let us break their bands asunder,
>   And cast away their cords from us."

They trust in chariots and in horses; their kings think
that they will be saved by the multitude of their hosts.
They inspire fear through the hearts of Israel, so that the
land trembles as though God had rent it, and the people
drink the wine of staggering and dismay. So tremendous
is their assault, so overwhelming their numbers, that all
help of man seems vain.

It is thus in every era of the history of God's people that
Satan has stirred up their foes. Right behind the coalitions
of men lies the malignity of the fallen spirit, who ever seeks
to bruise the heel of the woman's seed. " In the world ye
shall have tribulation." " Behold, the devil shall cast some
of you into prison, that ye may be tried; and ye shall have
tribulation ten days." " When the dragon saw that he was
cast down to the earth, he persecuted the woman."

II. THE ATTITUDE OF FAITH.—While the serried ranks
of the foe are in sight, the hero-king is permitted a vision
into the unseen and eternal. There is no fear upon the
face of God, no change in his determination to set his king
upon his holy hill. In fact, it seems that the day of his
foes' attack is that in which he receives a new assurance of
sonship, and is bidden to claim the nations for his inheritance, and the uttermost parts of the earth for his possession.
As he anticipates the battle, he hears the chime of the
divine promise above the tumult of his fear:

> " Thou shalt break them with a rod of iron;
>   Thou shalt dash them in pieces like a potter's vessel."

On his leaving the capital his people pray that the Lord may answer him in the day of trouble, remember his offerings, and send him help from the sanctuary; and he replies:

> " I know that the Lord saveth his anointed;
>   He will answer him from his holy heaven
>   With the saving strength of his right hand."

He knows that through the loving-kindness of the Most High he shall not be moved, but that his right hand will destroy his enemies.

In the ecstasy of his faith he asserts, as he looks eastward across the Jordan, that Gilead will as certainly own his sway as Ephraim and Manasseh did. Strong in the allegiance of Judah and her sister tribes, he counts victory already secured. Moab is his washing-basin; Edom, like a slave, shall carry his shoes; Philistia shall tremble before his war-shout, and even the strong city of Petra shall receive his troops.

In perfect peace he anticipates the result: the Lord will send forth the rod of his strength out of Zion, and strike through kings in the day of his wrath, and make his enemies his footstool, so that in all after days he may combine the office of priest and king, as Melchizedek did on that same site centuries before.

III. THE WARRIORS OF THE PRIEST-KING.—Catching the contagion of his faith, they triumph in God's salvation, and in his name set up their banners. They believe that God, as a Man of War, is going forth with their hosts, and will tread down their adversaries. They are characterized by *the willingness of their service.* No mercenaries are

pressed into their ranks; they gladly gather around the
standard, as the warriors of whom Deborah sang, who
willingly offered themselves. *They are clad, not in mail,
but in the fine linen of the priests;* "the beauties of holi-
ness," a phrase which suggests that the warfare was conducted by religious men, as an act of worship to God.
They are numerous as the dewdrops that bespangle the
morning grass, when every blade has its own coronet of
jewels, and the light is reflected from a million diamonds
(Ps. cx.).

What an exquisite conception of David's ideal for his
soldiers, and of the knightly chivalry, of the purity, truth,
and righteousness, in which all the soldiers of the Messiah
should be arrayed!

IV. THE COMPLETENESS OF THE VICTORY.—The
armies of the alien cannot stand the onset of those heaven-
accoutred soldiers. Kings of armies flee apace. They are
bowed down and fallen in bitter, hopeless defeat. They
are made as a fiery furnace in the time of God's anger, and
swallowed up in his wrath. Their dead bodies strew the
battle-field, and the valleys are choked with slain.

As the triumphant army returns, leaving desolation where
their foes had swarmed, they express in song their gratitude
to their almighty Deliverer. Singers and minstrels, Benjamin and Judah, Zebulun and Naphtali, join in the mighty
anthem:

" God is unto us a God of deliverances;
   And unto Jehovah the Lord belong the issues from death.
   O God, thou art terrible out of thy holy places:
   The God of Israel, he giveth strength and power unto his people."

All this has a further reference. In David we have a
type of the Messiah. For, of a truth, against the holy

Servant Jesus, whom God has anointed, both the Gentiles and the peoples of Israel have gathered together. Men have refused his sway, and do refuse it; but God hath sworn, and will not repent, that to him every knee shall bow, and every tongue confess; and it is more sure than that to-morrow's sun will rise that, ere long, great voices shall be heard in heaven, saying, "The kingdoms of the world are become the kingdoms of our Lord, and of his Christ; and he shall reign for ever and ever" (Rev. xi. 15–18).

XXV

The Sin of his Life

(2 SAMUEL xi.–xix.)

> " O Father, I have sinned! I have done
>   The thing I thought I nevermore should do!
>   My days were set before me, light all through;
>   But I have made dark—alas, too true!—
> And drawn dense clouds between me and my Sun."
>
> SEPTIMUS SUTTON.

THE chronicler omits all reference to this terrible blot on David's life. The older record sets down each item without extenuation or excuse. The gain for all penitents would so much outweigh the loss to the credit of the man after God's own heart. These chapters have been trodden by myriads who, having well-nigh lost themselves in the same dark labyrinth of sin, have discovered the glimmer of light by which the soul may pass back into the day: "Thy sins, which are many, are forgiven thee; go in peace."

I. THE CIRCUMSTANCES THAT LED TO DAVID'S SIN. —The warm poetic temperament of the king specially exposed him to a temptation of this sort; but the self-restrained habit of his life would have prevailed had there not been some slackening of the loin, some failure to trim the lamp.

For seventeen years he had enjoyed an unbroken spell

193

cf prosperity; in every war successful, on every great occasion increasing the adulation of his subjects. This was fraught with peril. The rigors of the Alps are less to be dreaded than the heat of the enervating plains of the Campagna.

In direct violation of the law of Moses—which forbade the multiplication of wives on the part of Hebrew kings, "lest their hearts should turn away"—we are distinctly told that, when established at Jerusalem, David took unto him more concubines and wives; sowing to himself the inevitable harvest of heart-burning jealousy, quarreling, and crime, of which the harem must always be the prolific source, besides fostering in David himself a habit of sensual indulgence, which predisposed him to the evil solicitation of that evening hour.

He had also yielded to a fit of indolence, unlike the martial spirit of the Lion of Judah; allowing Joab and his brave soldiers to do the fighting around the walls of Rabbah, while he tarried still at Jerusalem. It was a mood to which Uriah administered a stinging rebuke when he refused to go to his own house while his comrades and the ark were encamped on the open field.

One sultry afternoon the king had risen from his afternoon siesta, and was lounging on his palace roof. In that hour of enervated ease, to adopt Nathan's phrase, a traveler came to him, a truant thought, to satisfy whose hunger he descended into the home of a poor man and took his one ewe lamb, although his own folds were filled with flocks. We will not extenuate his sin by dwelling on Bathsheba's willing complicity, or on her punctilious ceremonial purification, while she despised her plighted married troth to her absent husband. The Scripture record lays the burden of the sin on the king alone, before whose absolute power Bathsheba may have felt herself obliged to yield.

One brief spell of passionate indulgence, and then—his character blasted irretrievably; his peace vanished; the foundations of his kingdom imperiled; the Lord displeased; and great occasion given to his enemies to blaspheme! Let us beware of our light, unguarded hours. Moments of leisure are more to be dreaded than those of strenuous toil. Middle life—for David was above fifty years of age —has no immunity from temptations and perils which be-set the young. One false step taken in the declension of spiritual vigor may ruin a reputation built up by years of religious exercise.

A message came one day to David from his companion in sin that the results could not be hidden. It made his blood run with hot fever. The law of Moses punished adultery with the death of each of the guilty pair. Instant steps must be taken to veil the sin! Uriah must come home! He came, but his coming did not help the matter. He refused to go to his home, though on the first night the king sent him thither a mess of meat straight from his table, and on the second made him drunk. The chivalrous soul of the soldier shrank even from the greeting of his wife while the great war was still in progress.

There was no alternative but that he should die; for dead men tell no tales. If a child was to be born, Uriah's lips, at least, should not be able to disown it. He bore to Joab, all unwitting, the letter which was his own death-warrant. Joab must have laughed to himself when he got it: "This master of mine can sing psalms with the best; but when he wants a piece of dirty work done, he must come to me. He wants to rid himself of Uriah—I won-der why? Well, I'll help him to it. At any rate, he will not be able to say another word to me about Abner. I shall be able to do almost as I will. He will be in my power henceforth." Uriah was set in the forefront of the hottest battle, and left to die; the significant item of his death being inserted in the bulletin sent to the king from the camp.   It was supposed by David that only he and Joab knew of this thing; probably Bathsheba did not guess the costly method by which her character was being protected.   She lamented for her dead husband, as was the wont of a Hebrew matron, congratulating herself, meanwhile, on the fortunate coincidence; and within seven days was taken into David's house   A great relief this!   The child would be born under the covert of lawful wedlock! There was one fatal flaw, however, in the whole arrangement: "The thing that David had done displeased the Lord."   David and the world were to hear more of it. But oh, the bitter sorrow that he who had spoken of walking in his house with a perfect heart, with all his faculty for divine fellowship, with all the splendid record of his life behind him, should have fallen thus!   The psalmist, the king, the man, the lover of God, all trampled in the mire by one dark, wild, passionate outburst!   Ah me!   My God, grant that I may finish my course without such a rent, such a blot!   Oh to wear the white flower of a blameless life to the end!

II. DELAYED REPENTANCE.—The better the man the dearer the price he pays for a short season of sinful pleasure.   For twelve whole months the royal sinner wrapped his sin in his bosom, pursed his lips, and refused to confess. But in the Thirty-second Psalm he tells us how he felt. His bones waxed old through his roaring all the day long. He was parched with fever heat, as when in Israel for three years there was neither dew nor rain in answer to Elijah's prayer, and every green thing withered in the awful drought of summer.   Day and night God's hand lay heavily upon him.

When he took Rabbah, he treated the people with ferocious cruelty, as if weary of his own remorse, and expending on others the hardness which he ought to have dealt out to himself. We often excuse ourselves from avenging our own sin by our harsh behavior and uncharitable judgments toward others. The same spirit which always characterizes the sullen, uneasy conscience flamed out in his sentence on the rich man who had taken the poor man's lamb. The Levitical law in such a case only adjudged fourfold restoration (Exod. xxii. 1). The king pronounced sentence of death.

Nathan's advent on the scene must have been a positive relief. One day, while statesmen and soldiers were crowding the outer corridor of the cedar palace, the prophet, by right of old acquaintance, made his way through them, and sought a private audience. He told what seemed to be a real and pathetic story of high-handed wrong; and David's anger was greatly kindled against the man who had perpetrated it. Then, as a flash of lightning on a dark night suddenly reveals to the traveler the precipice on the void of which he is about to place his foot, the brief, awful, stunning sentence, "Thou art the man!" revealed David to himself in the mirror of his own judgment, and brought him to his knees. Nathan reminded him of the past, and dwelt specially on the unstinted goodness of God. It was a sunny background, the somber hues of which made recent events look the darker. "Thou hast despised his word; thou hast slain Uriah; thou hast taken his wife. The child shall die; thy wives shall be treated as thou hast dealt with his; out of thine own house evil shall rise against thee." "I have sinned against the Lord," was David's only answer—a confession followed by a flood of hot tears, and instantly his scorched heart found relief. O blessed showers that visit parched souls and parched lands!

When Nathan had gone he beat out that brief confession into the Fifty-first Psalm, dedicated to the chief musician, that all the world might use it, setting it to music if they would.   The one sin and the many transgressions; the evil done against God, as though even Uriah might not be named in the same breath; the confession of inbred evil; the ache of the broken bones; the consciousness of the unclean heart; the loss of joy; the fear of forfeiting the Holy Spirit; the broken and contrite heart—thus the surcharged waters of the inner lake broke forth turbid and dark.   Ah, those cries for the multitude of God's tender mercies! Nothing less could erase the dark legend from the book of remembrance, or rub out the stains from his robe, or make the leprous flesh sweet and whole.   To be clean, because purged with hyssop; to be whiter than snow, because washed; to sing aloud once more, because delivered from blood-guiltiness; to be infilled with a steadfast, a willing, and a holy spirit; to be able to point transgressors to the Father's heart—these were the petitions which that weak, sin-weary heart laid upon the altar of God, sweeter than burnt-offering or fragrant incense.

But long before this pathetic prayer was uttered, immediately on his acknowledgment of sin, without the interposition of a moment's interval between his confession and the assurance, Nathan had said, "The Lord hath put away thy sin."

" I acknowledged my sin unto thee, and mine iniquity have I not hid.
    I said, I will confess my transgressions unto the Lord;
    And thou forgavest the iniquity of my sin."

Penitent soul! dare to believe in the instantaneous forgiveness of sins.   Thou hast only to utter the confession to find it interrupted with the outbreak of the Father's love. As soon as the words of penitence leave thy lips they are met by the hurrying assurances of a love which, while it hates sin, has never ceased to yearn over the prodigal.

Sin is dark, dangerous, damnable; but it cannot stanch the love of God; it cannot change the love that is not of yesterday, but dates from eternity itself. The only thing that can really hurt the soul is to keep its confession pent within itself. If only with stuttering, broken utterance it dares to cry, " Be merciful to me, the sinner, for the sake of the blood that was shed," it instantly becomes white as snow on Alpine peaks; pure as the waters of mid-ocean, which the stain of the great city cannot soil; transparent as the blue ether which is the curtain of the tabernacle of the Most High.

XXVI

The Stripes of the Children of Men

(2 SAMUEL xii.–xix.)

" No action, whether foul or fair,
　Is ever done, but it leaves somewhere
　A record written by fingers ghostly,
　As a blessing or a curse, and mostly
　In the greater weakness or greater strength
　Of the acts which follow it."

LONGFELLOW.

SIN may be forgiven, as David's was, and yet a long
train of sad consequences ensue. The law of cause
and effect will follow on, with its linked chain of disaster;
though God's mercy to his erring and repentant children
will be shown in converting the results of their sin into the
fires of their purification; in setting alleviation of the tenderest sort against their afflictions; and in finally staying
the further outworking of evil. All these facts stand out
upon the pages which tell the story of God's chastisements,
alleviations, and deliverance.

O soul of man, this is solemn reading for us; it is the
inner story of God's dealing with his own. As he dealt
with David he will deal with us. He will forgive, but he
may have to use the rod; he may restore to his favor, and
yet permit us to drink the bitter waters which our sin has
tapped. Be meek, patient, and submissive; thou wilt come
forth out of the ordeal a white soul, and men shall learn

through thy experiences the goodness and severity of God. Forgiven men may have to reap as they have sown.

I. GOD'S CHASTISEMENTS.—Bathsheba's little child was very sick. It was the child of sin and shame, but the parents hung over it; for seven days the mother watched it, and the father fasted and lay on the earth. He suffered more in seeing the anguish of the babe than if ten times its pain had been inflicted on himself. It cuts to the quick when the innocent suffer for our crimes. On the seventh day the child died.

Two years after, one of his sons treated his sister as David had treated Uriah's wife. They say a man never hears his own voice till it comes back to him from the phonograph. Certainly a man never sees the worst of himself until it reappears in his child. In Amnon's sin David beheld the features of his own unbridled passions; and in his murder by Absalom, two years after, David encountered again his own blood-guiltiness. Absalom's fratricide would never have taken place if David had taken instant measures to punish Amnon. But how could he allot that penalty to his son's impurity which he had evaded for himself? (Lev. xviii. 9–29). Nor could he punish Absalom for murder, when he remembered that he, a murderer, had eluded the murderer's fate.

When presently Absalom's rebellion broke out, it received the immediate sanction and adherence of David's most trusty counselor, whose advice was like the oracle of God. What swept Ahithophel into the ranks of that great conspiracy? The reason is given in the genealogical tables, which show that he was the grandfather of Bathsheba, and that his son Eliam was the comrade and friend of Uriah.

It is thought by some that at this time David was smitten with some severe form of disease. The Forty-first and Fifty-fifth psalms are supposed to record his sufferings during these dreary years. They tell the tale of his depression, depict the visitors that surrounded his bed, and recount the comments they passed on the sick man.

The most disastrous and terrible blow of all was the rebellion of Absalom. His beautiful figure, ready wit, apparent sympathy with the anxieties and disappointments of the people fretting under the slow administration of the law; his sumptuous expenditure and splendor—all these had for four years been undermining David's throne, and stealing away the hearts of the people, so that, when he erected his standard at Hebron, and was proclaimed king throughout the land, it was evident that the people had lost their former reverence and love for David—perhaps the story of his sin had disappointed and alienated them, and they hurried to pay their homage at the shrine of the new prince.

We need not recount the successive steps of those stormy days: the panic-stricken flight of the king: "Arise, and let us flee: make speed to depart;" the barefoot ascent of Olivet; the anguish that wept with loud voice; the shameful cursing of Shimei; the apparent treachery of Mephibosheth; the humiliation of David's wives in the sight of that which had witnessed his own sin; the gathering of all Israel together unto Absalom in apparent oblivion of the ties which for so many years had bound them to himself.

Such were the strokes of the Father's rod that fell thick and fast upon his child. They appeared to emanate from the malignity and hate of man; but David looked into their very heart, and knew that the cup which they held to his lips had been mixed by Heaven, and that they were not the punishment of a Judge, but the chastisement of a Father.

Outside the story of Christ there is nothing in the Bible

more beautiful than his behavior as he passed through this tangled growth of thorns. " Carry back the ark of God," he said to Zadok; "he may bring me again to see both it and his habitation; but if not, behold, here am I, let him do to me as seemeth good unto him." And when Shimei, perhaps referring to the recent execution of the sons of Rizpah, and perhaps suggesting that he had been guilty of the death of Ishbosheth, called him a man of blood because of his dealings with Saul's house, David said to Abishai, "The Lord hath permitted him to curse; and who shall say, Wherefore hast thou done so?" Thus, when Judas brought the bitter cup to the lips of Christ, the Master said, "It is the cup my Father hath given me to drink." Let us never forget the lesson. Pain and sorrow may be devised against us by the malignity of an Ahithophel, a Shimei, or a Judas; but if God permits such things to reach us, by the time that they have passed through the thin wire of his sieve they have become his will for us; and we may look up into his face and know that we are not the sport of chance or wild misfortune or human caprice, but are being trained as sons. Without such chastisement we might fear that we were bastards.

II. GOD'S ALLEVIATIONS.—They came in many ways. The bitter hour of trial revealed a love on the part of his adherents of which the old king may have become a little oblivious.

Ahithophel's defection cut him to the quick. He tells the story in the psalms we have mentioned. His sensitive nature winced to think that the man of his friendship, in whom he trusted, and who did eat of his bread, had lifted up his heel against him; but then Hushai the Archite came to meet him with every sign of grief, and was willing, as his friend, to plead in the council-chamber of Absalom.

Shimei might curse him; but Ittai, the stranger, a man of Gath, with all his men, swore allegiance for life or death.

Zadok and Abiathar are there with the ark, their ancient animosity forgotten in their common sorrow for their master; Ziba meets him with summer fruits, clusters of raisins, and loaves of bread; Shobi and Machir and Barzillai make abundant provision for his hungry, weary, and thirsty followers; his people tell him that he must not enter the battle, because his life is priceless, and worth ten thousand of theirs.

It was as though God stooped over that stricken soul, and as the blows of the rod cut long furrows in the sufferer's back, the balm of Gilead was poured into the gaping wounds. Voices spoke more gently; hands touched his more softly; pitiful compassion rained tender assurances about his path; and, better than all, the bright-harnessed angels of God's protection encamped about his path and his lying down.

Thus he came to sing some of his sweetest songs, and among them the Third, Fourth, Sixty-first, Sixty-second, Sixty-third, and One Hundred and Forty-third psalms.

The two former are his morning and evening hymns, when his cedar palace was exchanged for the blue canopy of the sky. He knows that he has many adversaries, who say, "There is no help for him in God;" but he reckons that he is well guarded:

> "Thou, O Lord, art a shield about me;
> My glory, and the lifter up of mine head."

He is not afraid of ten thousands of the people; he lies down in peace to sleep, and awakes in safety, because the Lord sustains him. He knows that the Lord hath set him apart for himself, and feels that the light of his face will put more gladness into his heart than the treasures of the kingdom which he seemed to have forfeited forever.

Then, from the drought-smitten land which they were obliged to traverse, his soul thirsts to see the power and glory of God, as he had seen them in the sanctuary; and already he realizes perfect satisfaction. To long for God is to find him; to thirst after him is to feel the ice-cold water flowing over the parched lips. With these came a clear prevision of the issue of the terrible strife:

> " The king shall rejoice in God;
> Every one that sweareth by him shall glory:
> But the mouth of them that speak lies shall be stopped."

III. God's Deliverance.—The raw troops that Absalom had so hastily mustered were unable to stand the shock of David's veterans, and fled. Absalom himself was despatched by the ruthless Joab, as he swayed from the arms of the huge terebinth. The pendulum of the people's loyalty swung back to its old allegiance, and they eagerly contended for the honor of bringing the king back. Even the men of Judah, conscious of having forfeited his confidence by so readily following Absalom, repented, and urged him to return. Shimei cringed at his feet. Mephibosheth established his unfaltering loyalty. Barzillai was bound to the royal house forever by his profuse acknowledgments and the royal offers to Chimham. All seemed ending well.

One unfortunate occurrence delayed the peaceful conclusion of the whole matter. The ten tribes were greatly irritated that Judah had made and carried through all the arrangements for the king's return, and gave vent to hot, exasperating words. These the men of Judah answered with equal heat. At an inopportune moment Sheba sounded the trumpet of sedition, and raised the cry that was destined in the days of Rehoboam again to rend the land: " Every man to his tents, O Israel." The ten tribes immediately seceded, and another formidable revolt yawned at David's feet; and it was only put down by incredible exertions on the part of Joab. The death of Sheba was the last episode in this rebellion. It was quelled in blood, but always left a scar and seam in the national life.

Many were the afflictions of God's servant, but out of them all he was delivered. When he had learned the lesson the rod was stayed. He had been chastened with the rod of men, and with the stripes of the children of men; but God did not take away his mercy from him as from Saul; his house, his throne and kingdom, in spite of many conflicting forces, being made sure. Thus always—the rod, the stripes, the chastisements; but amid all the love of God, carrying out its redemptive purpose, never hasting, never resting, never forgetting, but making all things work together till the evil is eliminated and the soul purged. Then the afterglow of blessing, the calm ending of the life in a serene sundown.

XXVII

𝕾unset and 𝕰vening 𝕾tar

(1 CHRONICLES xx.–xxix.)

" Sunset and evening star,
  And one clear call for me ;
And may there be no moaning of the bar
  When I put out to sea!"

TENNYSON.

A PERIOD of ten years of comparative repose was granted David between the final quelling of the revolts of Absalom and Sheba and his death. The recorded incidents of those years are few. It is probable that David walked softly and humbly with God, not minding high things, and concentrating his attention on the erection of the temple, which had been the dream of his life. If he might not build it himself, he would strive with all his might to help him who will.

I. ITS SITE.—This was indicated in the following manner. He conceived the design of numbering Israel and Judah. The chronicler says that Satan moved him to it, while the older record attributes the suggestion to the anger of the Lord. It is not impossible to reconcile these two statements, since the Old Testament writers so frequently attribute to God's agency what we would refer to his permissive providence.

The sin of numbering the people probably lay in its motive. David was animated by a spirit of pride and vainglory. He was eager to make a fine show among the surrounding nations, and impress them with a conception of Israel's greatness, so that they might not dare to attack any point on the long frontier line. There was a tendency to exchange his chosen position of waiting only on God, and to trust in the arm of human prowess and organization.

In spite of the remonstrances of Joab and others, the king persisted; and the officers went to and fro throughout the land, taking the sum of the people. Truly the nation had grown vastly since it was a scattered, demoralized remnant after the defeat of Gilboa. Excluding the tribes of Levi and Benjamin, and the city of Jerusalem, the fighting men of Israel numbered about a million, and those of Judah five hundred thousand.

When the enumeration was nearly complete, and the officers had reached Jerusalem, David's heart smote him, and he said unto the Lord, "I have sinned greatly in that I have done." He saw how far he had swerved from the idea of the theocracy, in which God's sovereignty alone determined the nation's policy. He had substituted his own whim for the divine edict, and had involved himself and his people in the charge of emulating the kings and nations around. A night of anguish could not, however, wipe out the wrong and folly of nine months. He might be forgiven, but must submit to one of three modes of chastisement. It was wise on his part to choose to fall into the hands of God; but the plague which devastated his people with unparalleled severity cut him to the quick.

Sweeping through the country, it came at last like a destroying army to the Holy City; and it seemed to be the Angel of the Lord hovering over it, sword in hand, to begin his terrible commission. Then it was that David cried

unto the Lord, pleading that his judgments might be
stayed: "Better let thy sword be plunged into my heart,
than that one more of my people should perish. I have
done perversely; but these sheep, what have they done?"
And the Angel of the Lord stayed by the threshing-floor
of Araunah, or Ornan, a Jebusite, who is thought by some
to have been the deposed king of the old Jebusite city.
There, on Mount Moriah, where centuries before the angel
had stayed the uplifted knife of Abraham, God said, "It
is enough; stay thine hand." That spot became the site
of the temple. At the direction of the prophet Gad,
David purchased the threshing-floor, the threshing instruments, and the oxen that trod out the grain. He insisted
on paying the full price, that he might not give God that
which cost him nothing; and thenceforward Mount Moriah
became the center of national worship, the site of successive temples, and the scene of the manifestation of the Son
of man.

II. Its Builder.—The last year of David's life, and
the fortieth of his reign, was embittered by a final revolt
of the discordant elements which had so often given him
trouble. Joab at last turned traitor to his old master; and
Abiathar, instigated probably by jealousy of Zadok, joined
him in espousing the cause of Adonijah, the eldest surviving son. They must have known God's distinct assurance
that Solomon was his chosen king; but they realized that
there was little hope of being intrusted with his confidence,
and therefore resolved on making one last effort to set him
aside and foist on the nation a nominee of their own.

When the account of the revolt was brought to David,
it stirred the old lion-heart, and though he had reached the
extreme point of physical exhaustion, he aroused himself
with a flash of his former energy to take measures for the

execution of the divine will communicated to him years
before. " And the king sware, and said, As the Lord liv-
eth, who hath redeemed my soul out of all adversity, as I
sware unto thee, so will I do." Not many hours passed
before tidings broke in on Adonijah's feast at Enrogel, to
say that Solomon had been anointed king in Gihon, by
the hand of Zadok, the priest, and Nathan, the prophet, and
had ridden through the city on the royal mule, escorted by
Benaiah and his men-at-arms. Within an hour the whole
of Adonijah's supporters had melted away, and he was
clinging, as a fugitive, to the horns of the altar.

It was probably about this time that David gave Solomon the charge to build the house for God. He recapitu-
lated the steps by which he had been led; from his desire
to build the house, and the divine refusal on account of his
having shed so much blood, to the divine assurance that a
son should be born who should be a man of rest and
should build the temple of peace. He then enumerated
the treasures he had accumulated, and the preparatory
works which had been set on foot. It is almost impossible
for us to realize the immense weight of precious metal, the
unlimited provision of brass, iron, and timber, or the armies
of workmen. The surrounding countries had been drained
of their wealth and stores to make that house exceedingly
magnifical.

At the close of this solemn charge he added instructions
to direct Solomon in his behavior toward Joab and Shimei.
These have the appearance of vindictiveness; but we must
give the dying monarch credit for being animated with a
single purpose for the peace of the realm. Had vengeance
been in his heart he might have taken it forthwith.

III. Its Pattern.—The Jewish polity required that the
king should not only be anointed by the priest, but recog-

nized by the entire people. It was therefore necessary
that David's choice should be ratified in a popular assembly, which gathered at the royal command (1 Chron.
xxviii. 1). What an august spectacle must that have been
when for the last time the aged king stood face to face
with the men who had helped to make Israel great, many
of whom had followed him from comparative obscurity!
It resembled the farewell of Moses to the people whom he
had led to the threshold of Canaan; or Samuel's parting
address. For the last time monarch and people stood together before God. Again he recited the circumstances of
his choice, of his desire to build the temple, and the substi-
tution of Solomon for himself. Then, turning to the stripling that stood beside him, he bade him be strong and
carry out the divine purpose.

Next followed the gift of the pattern of all the house
which had been communicated to David by the Spirit of
God, and an inventory of the treasures from which each
article was to be constructed. As Moses saw the Land of
Promise gleam before his dying gaze, so to David's imagination the splendid temple stood forth in every part complete. The contribution from his private fortune had been
most munificent; and with this as his plea he turned to the
vast concourse, asking princes and people to fill their hands
with gifts. The response was splendid. It is probable
that never before or since has such a contribution been
made at one time for religious purposes; but, better than
all, the gifts were made willingly and gladly.

With a full heart David blessed the Lord before all the
congregation. His lips were touched with the olden fire;
his thoughts expanded beneath the warmth of his imagination, and rose to heaven; he ascribed to Jehovah the
universal kingdom, and recognized that all which had been
contributed that day had been first received. Standing

upon the threshold of the other world, his days seemed as a shadow in which there was no abiding; and then the king and father pleaded for Solomon, that he might keep the divine statutes and build the house.   Next he turned to the people, and bade them join in ascriptions of praise; and there went forth such a shout of jubilation, of blessing and praise, that the welkin rang again; while a great religious festival crowned the proceedings.

It was a worthy conclusion to a great life!   How long after David lingered we cannot tell.   Sacred historians do not expend their words in describing dying scenes.   One record says simply that " David slept with his fathers, and was buried in the city of David;" another that "he died in a good old age, full of days, riches, and honor."   But perhaps the noblest is that uttered by the Holy Spirit through the lips of Paul: " David, after he had served his own generation according to the will of God, fell on sleep, and saw corruption."

It is beautiful to find that word *sleep* used of David's death.   His life had been full of tumult, storm, and passion, of war and blood; many a revolt had cast its foam in his face; but rest came at last, as it will come to all.   Like a tired infant's, those aged eyes closed in the last sleep, and the spirit joined the mighty dead.   His sepulcher remained to the day of Pentecost, for Peter refers to it; but the man whom God had raised up was drinking of the river of his pleasures, and was satisfied as he awoke in his likeness.   The fairest dreams of his Lord that had ever visited his soul fell short of the reality; and upon his aged face must have rested a look of glad surprise, as though the half had not been told.

The parallel between him and our Lord may be carried into minute particulars.   In their anointing; their inimitable words; their sufferings; their zeal for the house of

God; their love for their friends; their betrayal by those they had trusted; their wars; their love for Jerusalem— how much in common! But there the parallel stays. In his atoning death, in his incorruptible nature, in his glorious ascension, the Son of David stands alone. David himself, in the Spirit, called him Lord, and knew that he alone could fulfil that ideal of kingship which had passed before his inspired thought, given to him by the Holy Ghost, but which no mere mortal would ever be able to realize.

> " For he shall come down like rain upon the mown grass:
> As showers that water the earth.
> He shall have dominion also from sea to sea,
> And from the river to the ends of the earth.
> He shall deliver the needy when he crieth;
> And the poor that hath no helper.
> His name shall be continued as long as the sun:
> And men shall be blessed in him."

Printed in the United States of America.